# ABUSE
## *No More*

KEYS TO FREEDOM FROM ABUSE

*Teena Louise Rawding*

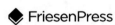 FriesenPress

Suite 300 – 990 Fort St
Victoria, BC, V8V 3K2
Canada

www.friesenpress.com

Unless otherwise noted, Scripture quotations are taken from the King James Version.

teenarawding.com
abusenomore3keys@gmail.com
www.teerawd-vw.wixsite.com/mysite

ISBN
978-1-5255-2601-5 (Hardcover)
978-1-5255-2602-2 (Paperback)
978-1-5255-2603-9 (eBook)

*1. BODY, MIND & SPIRIT, HEALING, PRAYER & SPIRITUAL*

Distributed to the trade by The Ingram Book Company

This book is dedicated to the memory of
a most beautiful, caring, and loving young lady,
Nayana Lacasse
1978-2018

There is no greater victory for a victim of abuse then to realize that they've got what it takes. Daniel has done that by simply loving me just the way I am. He acknowledges my simplest thoughts, laughed and cried with all my pages, and even validates my stuttering.

Our Lord saved the best Wine for Last at the marriage feast, and shared wine with His disciples at the last supper. "We won't drink again until we meet in Glory," He said.

Daniel and I have been served the best wine last, finding happiness even in our latter years.

# TABLE OF CONTENTS

## Credit to

Much credit to my wonderful husband, Daniel. He is my lover, encourager and best friend. He has been my spiritual mentor and leader since the day I met him, and he has spoken only positive words and blessings over me and my work of writing.

Although I wrote the book, I hope to have learned from his wealth of knowledge and close walk with the Lord. Some of it I hope has rubbed off on me to write just a little bit better due to knowing him.

Much credit to each of my four children whom I call my soldiers, my angels. They are walking both sides of the fence, in love; and they have to be soldier and angel to be able to balance that. God bless you and your families.

Blessings and thanks to all my large family who have been there for me much more than I have been there for them. May God give you a double portion.

# This Book

There are many articles and books on domestic abuse in bookstores or on line. There are medical reasons that explain very well such sicknesses as depression, Post-traumatic Stress disorder (PTSD), Obsessive Compulsive Disorder, (OCD), Obsessive Compulsive Personality Disorder (OCPD), narcissism, Schizophrenia and the list goes on. But this book is not about the medical reasons why abusers do what they do.

Even Christian bookstores can carry books too technical and complicated for someone victimized by abuse to read and understand.

These pages are done in a carefree, simple and down home style. One page at a time, for the victim of abuse that has only short bits of time for reading. I have written this in hopes it will be an arm around you and a heart that understands.

In actual life, growth and change happen in slow step-by-step processes, and I hope that in reading a page at a time, you will find comfort in your time of need, and eventually growth and understanding of God's mercy and love, especially in your times of trouble.

Read the pages slowly, and soak in what you have read. Feel free to write in it, scribble on it, vent, praise, laugh, and cry with the writer. No neatness required because real life is not neat.

I have often desired to solve the mystery of domestic abuse. It is a puzzling matter that the person you loved and married has become your enemy. They are the one in the whole world you fear the most.

They are the criminal that you sleep with. The person you would turn in to police, if they did on the street what they do at home. You have allowed this person to raise your children and you wonder, "How did it come to be?" The question isn't just how can the abuser do what he or she does, but how have you come so far away from what you yourself know to be right?

This is not to bash the abuser, nor yourself, because we are all a creation of God and we are all alike, sinners who need forgiveness and grace. There may be many reasons why some people have chosen to abuse the ones they love, but none of them are good enough for anyone to say that it is okay.

All stories of abuse have much in common, and many are very similar to others. Any stories related in this text are changed from how they were told to me or from what I might have experienced.

Divorce can be a very touchy subject if you are a Christian and believe that under no circumstance should divorce ever occur. You may find this book contradictory to scripture, but violence in a home is also contradictory to God's Word. Each person will at some point make their own decision as to how to deal with the situation. In the meantime, I hope this book will help you find direction and strength.

I hope you will be encouraged, will find your worth—even joy— in the midst of trials, to believe in yourself; to believe in God who created you just exactly the way you are; to be strengthened in your soul, in your mind and body; to become confident enough to make the big decisions for life's most difficult problems.

_____

_____

_____

_____

## The Brighter Side

God has been so good to me all along my journey in life.

Yes, there were many difficult years, but God was there with me and protecting me and my family.

In the midst of the most desperate years, there were always times of joy and times that stand out that the Lord especially surrounded me. Wonderful people were part of my life. People who smiled, dropped in for a quick visit, excused me for my awkwardness, gave loving compliments. Some did not know they were ministering as angels. I well remember a lady who brought me a beautifully cooked ham and a poppy seed cake to celebrate my new baby at that time. There were a few Pastors, some knowingly and some unaware of my situation, who gave me wise words of encouragement.

> *"And this day shall be unto you for a memorial; and ye shall keep it a feast to the LORD throughout your generations; ye shall keep it a feast by an ordinance forever." Exodus 12:14*

There are many stories in scripture that tell of how God told the people of Israel to gather stones and make a memorial to Him and to the remembrances of His deliverance so the message will be told and retold to the future generations of God's goodness. One of many can be read in Joshua 4.

Mark the good times even while you are dealing with the bad. You might not feel like you are giving a lot, but you are giving your life to your situation. God sees every little thing you give even in your emotional poverty. Matthew 10:42 – "… giving a cup of water to one of these little ones will not go unrewarded."

Though there were many grievous years living with a perfidious man, I choose to see the good that came out of such years. There were many markers along the way of how good God was to me. I did not always see it at the time, but later it became very apparent that I and my family had been carried by a Higher Power, the Lord Jesus Himself.

The Lord knew all the days for me to be in this place and also the appointed time for me to step out of it.

One encouragement I would give is to find the sparkles in life even in treacherous times. If not right in the moment, then later.

Be creative in your giving, during the trial years, and God will not forget your love sacrifices and gifts. "Surely blessing I will bless thee, and multiplying I will multiply thee." Hebrews 6:14.

I'd like to add a word of encouragement to my children. God kept you even when you didn't know it. The difficulties you have experienced as a young person have shaped you in a good way to be the caring, giving, and understanding people that you are. Also you have not become bitter but more discerning and wise due to the very thing that the devil meant for your destruction. God has always had good plans for you in spite of what Satan the devil tried to destroy.

> *"'For I know the plans I have for you,' declares the Lord, 'plans to prosper you and not to harm you, plans to give you hope and a future.'" Jeremiah 29:11 NIV*

# God's Love for the Difficult Person

This book is not to disown or discard a difficult spouse. God made all people and called His creation "good."

Among all the people God loves are the gossipers, thieves, murderers and all manner of evil doers. "For all have sinned and come short of the glory of God." Romans 3:23. We all need forgiveness in order to cross over into the heavens when our time comes to pass on. At that time, there will be no large sin or small sin. We are all likewise, sinners.

We do not have to stay in our sin but can be forgiven. Then we will be children of God, no matter how great your sins have been.

"For God so loved the world that He gave His only begotten son, that whosoever believeth on Him shall not perish but have everlasting life." John 3:16. "But ... as many as receive Him, to them he gave the power to become the sons of God, even to them that believe on His name." John 1:12

Once we have believed in Jesus and that His shed blood was for the forgiveness of our sins, we are forgiven and made right with God.

Now that we are made right with God and our sins are washed away, we learn to live, by God's power, a life pleasing to Him. Some understand quickly that God has done it all and we need only believe and be filled with joy and walk in His light and power He gives to us every day.

Others, which would be most of us, want to get in there and live for Christ in our own strength. Many different things happen when we try this. When we try and fail we may get discouraged. We may get so tired of trying to be a Christian that we quit altogether. We may even raise ourselves above others if we think we are doing extremely well at this Christian thing. Living the Christian life on our own lacks the power of God and becomes a bunch of rules and often ends up being an act and not real.

Many abusers love rules and regulations and love being this kind of Christian. They think it is enough to act Christian in public and that they can abuse their family at home. They may hear a good sermon, twist it all into rules and laws and go home after church and demand stricter obedience from their spouse and family.

We all make mistakes and are hard to live with sometimes, but abusers make it eternally more difficult than most. Often they mix the good with the bad so much it causes great confusion. Sometimes their partner or spouse and their children, simply can't remain living with them.

God so loved the world that He sent His son to die for people's sins. Even for the abuser. You may not be able to live with such a person, but pray that they will repent of their sins and truly know what it is to be saved

_____

_____

_____

_____

_____

# A Day in the Life of a Victim of Domestic Abuse

"Which day should I write about?" she asked. "Which day should live on in my story? Should it be the day when my parents visited soon after the wedding?" The guests slept in the marriage bed while the newlyweds slept on the couch. That is how it was done in those days.

In the morning, her parents still sleeping soundly in the next room, her and her husband were having one of their first serious fights. He blamed her for letting him sleep in and be late for work. Before she knew what was happening she was on the floor, her head spinning from what just happened. She was to realize this morning that such things would always be her fault. She would decide many times over the years that she would work harder at being a better wife. It would prove in the end to be wrong thinking.

"Or", she thought, "Maybe I should speak of the time my third baby was born." Her mother-in-law had stayed a week to help out, but now she was gone. All had appeared peaceful as long as his mommy was around, but as soon as she had left, all hell broke loose.

She was far from having her full strength back, but it was expected of her to pull her full load by this time. She had noticed by now that all her in-laws were so strong. They all seemed to work like nothing had happened to them after each childbirth. It was life as usual at their houses: cooking, cleaning, keeping immaculate houses. Their babies always appeared to be well looked after and contented most of the time. Maybe there was really something wrong with her. Her husband's expectations might not be so far-fetched after all. But whatever she did, it was never enough.

Two little children to tend and a newborn baby to nurse and take care of; it kept her busy and running. Just as her husband walked in the door, on this particular day, a lamp tipped over by her baby girl who was only one, and there were a few toys on the couch and still some crumbs on the table from lunch. This was not acceptable to the man who walked through the door. The angry face plunged into a rage seeing the lamp on the side and broken. The outrage began thus and continued all through supper and evening. There was nothing she could say in her weakened state but it continued.

She cried and yelled and eventually didn't care how sick she was, she joined in the shouting and hitting match. Whimpering and then shouting again. The children needed care and the baby too, but the name calling and swearing continued. Hateful words, wishing the other dead. She didn't know how she ended up putting the two little ones to bed and the baby taken care of. This is how her children would grow up.

She wanted to phone someone but when there was just a moment where she could have done so, she didn't know who to phone. All she would have done was wail into the phone anyway, so she didn't want to do that.

Then when she had no more strength she got quiet. In one last burst of fury she, like an animal, started biting into her new yellow nightgown and tore it to shreds. How would her poor children make it through life with such parents? Then she fell back to bed broken. He demanded she put the night dress on, that was now full of holes, and she obeyed without a whimper. He then demanded apologies, which she quietly spoke.

"I'm sorry," she said in half a whisper. "I don't know what I was thinking." Then she obediently lay down on his bed and did as she was told. It was rape even though she had no strength to resist him.

She had no strength for any further altercation. He could not even wait for her to heal to be satisfied.

There were many other stories she could write, as she continued to contemplate all the days of all the years she lived with this abuser. Maybe she would write about all the times she walked out just to get some air, a break from the controller's incessant orders and criticisms, and all the 'how to's' and 'how not to's', and the hours or lectures on why and how to do every little bitty thing.

More times than not he followed her and caught up to her before she could have proper rest time for her brain.

Maybe she could tell of the times she planned how she would leave him. There were the attempts to escape that always eventually ended up back to square one. One of the times she ran off; she walked in the rain for hours and it felt so good. It was a small taste of freedom. But eventually she knew she needed to go back to her children.

She grudgingly walked back only to find the man who could torture her mentally and physically, now playing perfect father: cooking dinner and entertaining the children; cheerfully greeting her as she walked in, as if nothing had happened. This all making her wonder if she was crazy. Every attempt to walk or drive away always led her back to her prison home.

She did not know that she could raise her sweet and vulnerable little children alone, so she stayed. He had successfully brainwashed her into thinking she was completely insane and incapable of any normal tasks.

On the other hand, she continued to wonder, she could write about one of her writing days. "I'll write about that day I sat at the window in my immaculate home," she thought.

The sun was streaming into the dining room glass sliding door, across the table and over the vase of freshly-picked lilacs. Coffee was in her cup and a slice of toast and jam on a plate beside her. Maybe she should write about that day she thought. The children were now in school and the predictably violent man at work. Finally, she had time to write and all day to do it in.

Her solace in bad times was always that she would write it all down and someday the world would know the truth of her prison home and how it came to be so. Today she wanted to write it all down, every inch of it and figure it all out. This was not the first time she attempted to write what was happening. The secrets, the ugly secrets they were keeping behind tightly locked doors of what they called their home.

But on this beautiful day, she could not write anything. It was too terrible. Words jumbled over each other over her pages and nothing said it right. Faster and more furiously the words came but she was not satisfied. She tried and tried, and it became a jumble. She wrote so fast that after a while none of what she wrote was legible.

She decided to continue even though there was far too much to say all at once. The lines continued as scribbles, pages and pages of childish writing, line after line of wavy scribbles no longer words at all, and she did not care.

She was sure she was losing her mind as she often wondered, and yet her mind was not lost. She wrote for hours it seemed, and it seemed all for nothing. Finally, she stopped in deep depression. She was too tired to think anymore. Where were the real answers to her dilemma?

In desperation, she groped together all the crazy papers, tearing them into shreds. It was only worthy of the garbage bin, she thought. Maybe her life was only worthy of the garbage bin. All of it was just one big mountain of garbage, but now she was forced into another world.

She had to get her normal composure back and that poker smile pasted on her face before the children got home and more so before the dark face of the controller came through the door. If she even showed an ounce of discontent, he would notice and there would be more altercations. When these episodes started they did not end until she was completely ravenous of fresh air. None of her thoughts were clear and all were confusing but she must pretend all is well. No! She must believe that all is well.

She must be about her everyday business of keeping house and attending to children.

She could do it. She must do it.

_____

_____

_____

_____

_____

_____

_____

_____

_____

_____

_____

_____

_____

## Abuse No More!

What is abuse and when is it time to say, "It's enough!"?

Abuse is controlling behavior that is designed and crafted by the abuser to make another person dependent on them. They isolate them and use all manner of ways to brainwash their victim including instilling fear, through assaults, threats, and manipulations. Through incessant talking, being pushy, demanding, sneaky, using confusion, put-downs, criticisms; all to create self-doubt and terror in their victim. They seem to have no conscience and will use different forms of punishment to coerce the victim into doing exactly as told. They withhold the good, administer pain in different forms, being constantly on the lookout for faults and many terrorizing punishments.

Once they have you properly isolated and in a state of paralyzed terror, they began playing with your mind. They craft all different kinds of moods and evil threats so the victim never knows when and why there would be a violent outburst. They plan their so-called kindnesses alongside their disgusting evil.

Theirs is one of the most difficult crimes to figure out because they portray themselves so confident, smart, orderly, gracious, thoughtful, laughing, smiling, honest, and even humble. They simply have no conscience except for a crafted one that they put on like a mask and use at just the right time to impress.

They care only about themselves, and all they do, even the good, is for self-centered gain.

Abusers create a circular chase that keeps the victim scrambling. Fear of them is the worst thing because now they've got you. The fear causes your eyes to be on them and not on your own common sense and on what your own heart and soul tell you. The victim gets so tired of the chase that all they can think to do is to appease the demands of the abuser to find some relief. Relief is always short lived.

The only way this is ever going to stop is to expose the abuse. Stop your fear and put everything the abuser does into the public eye.

Some people live with abuse for many years. They simply don't know how to get out of the mental scramble they are in. Many die at the hands of the abuser. Some commit suicide as the only way out. Some simply get physically sick from the years of constant confusion and terror and die from their illnesses.

Those who live, may develop extreme low esteem, never knowing how to get free. Not believing they are capable of more. They live something of a zombie life and then they die. They have developed mental and emotional disorders that if not helped, will never be healed.

**If you find yourself in an abusive relationship, the sooner you get out the better.**

If you find yourself in an abusive relationship, the sooner you get out the better. Phone the doctor, the pastor, a trusted friend, neighbor, family member, or someone on a victim of abuse chat line.

Never say that your situation is not as bad as so and so's. If it's abuse, it is bad enough to go for help. Abuse can be like quicksand, the more you fight the more they close in on you. So, keep up your courage, be braver than you have ever been, keep your head about you, and go for help.

If you already feel like you have been swallowed up much like Jonah and the whale, cry to God. Put all religious beliefs aside and cry to the God of the Universe to help. The God of the Bible. The

God who loves you and can protect you and give you the strength you need.

> *"In my distress I called upon the LORD, and cried unto my God: he heard my voice out of his temple, and my cry came before him, even into his ears." Psalm 18:6*

_____

_____

_____

_____

_____

_____

_____

_____

_____

_____

# The Quick Fix

Some people like to live on quick fixes. Something that gives imme-diate relief but doesn't address the real problem. These have their purposes but in the long run, it's just the cane you can lean on but doesn't heal the crippling.

Where does abuse come from and why do people abuse? Many books, articles and blogs are written about this. Why do victims of abuse stay with their abusers? Why does the abuser look like the one that holds it all together and the victim look like they are dim witted? There are professional and medical terms for every possible cause but to learn them is only touching the surface. How does one decide which of the many solutions to apply and how to do it successfully?

The topic is so deep and wide, you would need a university degree to get to the bottom of it and then some. It might all be truthful but many victims of abuse don't have the energy to put one foot in front of the other, never mind doing a deep study of anything.

Only some victims become stronger after much time of taking care of themselves. They may come to a place where they do study their abuser, read books, gather much material that give information on abuse and so on, but does the abuser listen to what their spouse has learned? Not likely!

Some find temporary help involving 'chatting' with people online who have the same problems as they do. This can be helpful for a time. It is such a relief to find people who have the same problem as we do and to know that we aren't crazy. It may thrill us to death at first, but then after a while it is just going in circles and the same things are said every day. It becomes an angry outlet but never solves the real problem. A lot of talk, talk, talk. Finally one gets bored with it.

Support groups have their place. Talking to friends has its place, for a time, but often this has a short shelf life too. Eventually you need to do more.

So you may turn to religions of many kinds. More do's and don'ts. More programs to join. Temporary fixes. Memorizing clichés, good, but powerless of themselves. Personal counselling can be just what you need but a good counsellor knows that their patient needs to move on to healing, and the sessions must end at some point.

The real solution lies in Jesus and His Word. No, it is not a quick fix, although it can be the quickest fix imaginable. Ask anyone in AA how they overcame alcohol abuse. Ask anyone delivered from drugs how they did it. It always involves coming to the end of yourself. How did Corrie Ten Boom and her sister Betsy survive prison and war camps? Why were they not like many others who panicked and gnashed their teeth in bitterness and anger in their most desperate situations? Many testimonies of people come out of slums, out of the ghettos in New York, children beaten and abused and abandoned. Testimonies of some who have come out of anorexia, some who have escaped unbelievable abuses, some were delivered out of their situation, as if overnight, even in a moment. What is their testimony? It is always Jesus. No clichés or religion. No dos or don'ts, or more rules. Just a coming to the end of themselves and giving the whole mess to Jesus, humbly and completely sincerely.

There have been murderers who were raised from birth to hate and kill and working in governments as hit men, who were professional killers. One such person wrote a book: *Once an Arafat Man*. Tass Saada worked for Yasser Arafat, killing many people. He eventually becomes a born again Christian, and he is a changed man from the inside. Only Jesus can change a person's heart, even one who lived to murder.

This same Jesus can help the abuser and also the victim of abuse. Nobody can dictate who will come to the Lord Jesus Christ because it is each person's individual choice.

If you want a real life change and not just a temporary fix, you will become a believer in the God of Heaven and earth, the Creator God and Jesus Christ His Son, who loved the whole world so much He came to pay for all our sins. Follow the conviction of the Holy Spirit and you will find this Jesus.

> *"Wherefore he is able also to save them to the uttermost that come unto God by him, seeing he ever liveth to make intercession for them." Hebrews 7:25*

# A Penny for Your Thoughts

Every book should have some blank pages so that you could talk back to the writer about your thoughts on what you have read. You might have many ideas running through your mind. You might agree, disagree, include other ideas, or wish to delete what is written. The blank pages would help you do some interacting with the author whether you ever send it to the author or not.

You might wish more or less was said. Maybe there is some scripture you would include. Maybe a story or two that would fit perfectly could be added. It's often while we read that we would love something to be put in or taken out, but when the page is turned, it's out of mind what that important thought was. A blank page here and there would be great to remember all your great thoughts.

Usually a one-sided story gets boring after a while, whereas feedback helps the listener and the speaker both to get more out of the conversation. Don't you think every sermon at church should have some feedback time? Wouldn't we listen better and learn more if there was such a time set aside? It might well be that pastors don't do this because they are afraid of conflict or long-winded feedback, or afraid they wouldn't have the answers.

What a precious verse found in Revelation 3:20, "Behold, I stand at the door and knock. If any man hear my voice and open the door, I will come in to him, and sup with him and he with me."

The fellowship is one with another. Both are participants in this 'supping'.

In satisfying fellowship there is no haste. Don't you love it when someone listens to every word you say and asks questions that pertain to your topic? Then they share their own thoughts, which further inspires you.

True brainstorming works this way. When all feedback is positive, ideas are grown. Ideas that are original come out of such positive conversations. Listening and talking are both skills one can learn and get better at. There is also a time to be quiet and contemplate what has been said and what you will choose to say. Some people call them pregnant pauses. They are part of good communication. It is a good time to contemplate whether you heard and understood the next person's heart.

Jesus hears your thoughts and your heart. He communicates back to us if we listen closely. Sometimes He speaks words of encouragement through someone else, so keep your ears open for such blessings. In 1 Thessalonians we read, "Wherefore comfort yourselves together, and edify one another, even as also ye do." 1 Thessalonians 5:11

## Your Silence

Your silence is the abuser's greatest asset.

They may have succeeded to shut your mouth by using shame, put-downs and fears. Once this person can depend on those closest to them to keep the abuse quiet they've got it made. They can go about their crooked schemes without concern.

The abuser doesn't care that they have children and grandchildren, loving sons and daughters that have soft hearts. Young people who just want to believe that all will be well. Those who are willing to sacrifice beyond the call of duty to keep family in one piece and together.

Sometimes those in the family of abuse don't want to be involved so they look the other way. They are tired of the charade and just want to forget about this shameful cancer in their family. Who could blame them? It would take a lifetime and more to help an abuser so why the endless bother? That's how it goes with abusers. They never tire of their evil schemes. With the silence and secretiveness, the hopelessness in the family continues.

No! Break the silence! Do this as much as you can safely do. And as often as possible. Don't listen to people who want to protect the abuser. The only protection they need is to be exposed and then MAYBE they will see themselves and change. Bringing their shame into the light of day is the only help they need.

## If you think you can keep the peace by being quiet you are wrong.

If you think you can keep the peace by being quiet you are wrong. It is temporary and prolongs the bad situation. The abuser lets you think you have some control but you don't. They let you think you do, just so you stay a bit longer. You are tired of the waves. You are tired of the endless arguing that never has a peaceful closure. So you keep quiet. The bad news is that you are already in the muck up to your chin. To try to save yourself now by being quiet is absurd. The only way out of this relationship is through it and out the other end and be gone.

No, you never wanted this but it is too late. Don't be the dangling bait to thrill the one who has an evil mind. It is no shame to have made a mistake, to think the best of such a person, but also, it is no shame to change your mind and leave an abuser.

Don't cower in silence. Humble yourself and go for help as soon as it is safe. "He that covereth his sins shall not prosper: but whoso confesseth and forsaketh them shall have mercy." Proverbs 28:13

Covering shameful sin will not fix anything.

---

---

---

---

---

# I Will Do a New Thing

Fret not thyself because of evildoers, neither be thou envious against the workers of iniquity. For they shall soon be cut down like the grass, and wither as the green herb. Trust in the Lord, and do good; so shalt thou dwell in the land, and verily thou shalt be fed. Delight thyself also in the Lord: and he shall give thee the desires of thine heart. Commit thy way unto the Lord; trust also in him; and he shall bring it to pass. And he shall bring forth thy righteousness as the light, and thy judgment as the noonday. Psalm 37:1–6

Do you long for a new thing? A brand new thing to revive your soul? Are you tired of playing the obedient family dog? Are you tired of playing go fetch or playing sit, lie down, roll over? Are you tired of playing dead and then spring back to life the minute your master commands? A good dog will still eagerly go lick his master's feet after obeying all the master's commands. But you are not and never were a dog.

Your Higher Master, the Lord Jesus Christ will not demand of you what you cannot do. He will give you strength to do what He requires of you. Then as it says in Psalm 23:2, "He will make you to lie down in green pastures, and lead you beside still waters." He feeds His sheep. He takes good care of His own. He would die for His beloved sheep and He did. On the cross He gave His life. He shed His very blood. He was God and allowed himself to come to the lowest of the low and wash men's dirty feet. He did not hesitate to be humble.

He was not ashamed to be seen with Mary, a repentant prostitute, who wept at His feet and dried them with her hair. Then He died at the hands of unbelieving sinners and was mocked by His own people, the Jews. Such a person, could He not be trusted entirely? God in the flesh, we certainly can trust Him to give us what we need. To hear us and help us.

Give your life to Him, even if it is messed up, and He will do a new thing in you. He will raise you up from being treated like a dog. When you give yourself and your all to Him He will surprise you every day with new blessings and new mercies. Find a quiet place to talk to Him every morning. Don't make it a religion. Just go be with Jesus.

Walk to the park, or the river or in the woods, or go to a coffee shop near you to read your Bible in a quiet corner. Maybe all you can do is spend a few extra minutes in the bathroom and dedicate that time to being with the ONE who loves you more than anyone else here on earth. Build a relationship as you listen and sometimes talk, cry or whatever it is you want to do. He will help you have that NEW LIFE that we so long for.

_____

_____

_____

_____

_____

_____

## For the Beauty of the Earth

For the beauty of the earth,
For the beauty of the skies,
For the Love which from our birth,
Over and around us lies:
Christ, our God, to Thee we raise,
This our Sacrifice of Praise.

This hymn was written by Folliott S. Pierpoint (1835–1917). Some people live in constant fear and dread of a spouse who is demanding, selfish, and controlling. It takes a lot of hard work to live peaceably with such a person, if indeed it is at all possible.

When you lay it all out before God, He will give you many ways to still enjoy life, even when you are in a very difficult place. Those who wait on the Lord will "Fly like the eagle." Isaiah 40:31

If music is your thing, enjoy it whenever you can. Some may love reading, some are artsy, or maybe cooking is what you enjoy, or fishing, or dancing. If you put away your fear of your abuser and look at life more creatively, you will see times and places where you can let yourself enjoy at least some of the things that are to your liking. Nature walks can be most thrilling – you with your children or just you and your Loving Heavenly Father.

You may not have much time for yourself and these small enjoyments, but don't waste the few minutes that you do have. Use such moments to think up ways to bring joy to yourself or your children.

In your times of confined living, it is more important than ever to make use of the small bits of time you have, to build on the positive.

Maybe you like writing. Write your own book, tried and true, on how to live an abundant life even while with a controller. Christian bookstores lack such books. If you don't see how it will ever be published, don't worry about it. Write anyway.

As you walk close to the Lord, eventually you will be free from the abuser. You will be glad to look back and see that not all your time was wasted chasing after the empty wishes of your obsessive controller, that you still found value and a measure of peace and joy in the middle of chaos.

# Don't Die for the Wrong Cause

Do you have a martyr spirit? That is a gift. Do you put the needs of others above your own? Do you bend over backward so others can have what they want? This is a wonderful way to be, and many people will love you for it.

One trouble with that is that the controller spirit seeks you out. They have antennae out for you and can sense you from miles away. They have a hunger and thirst and a craving to control, like their life and breath depend on it. Like seeking their next breath, they seek you! They will court you and treat you like queens and kings, mesmerizing you with charms that will cause you to follow them to hell blindly and happily.

It makes for a great relationship when both parties have an understanding of trust. Every day can be a party whether you have riches or whether you live in a shack. Both people will just want to please and do it to a fault. They're happiest when the next person is happy. But should they fall into the wrong hands, they are done for!

The person who gives to a fault, needs to learn some boundaries in the sacrifices they make. When they give, then the controller takes, and keeps on taking. Controllers do not think like most people do. They have a different brain altogether. Although we seem to say the same things, the meaning of our words is completely different.

So be wise as a serpent and quietly remove yourself from such a person if you possibly can. If you are in over your head and that is not hard to do, then it will take a lot more to leave than you ever imagined. Remember, you are their next breath.

Only God can help you now. That is not a bad thing. That is where we need to go for help anyway, with all our needs; so this is a good place to start to get out of trouble. Pray hard when you are stuck. Pray hard when you feel used and abused. Praise hard when the abuser is out of sight. Praise and rely on your Loving Heavenly Father to be your rescuer.

God will help you but he will also ask something of you. One thing He will ask of you, that is to believe on Him. John 6:28–29. He will ask you to have faith in Him.

As you are learning to communicate with your Heavenly Father, to listen to Him, to talk with Him, you will have many opportunities to learn things on your way to rescue and recovery. You can become a better person even in the midst of this negative experience.

"When wisdom entereth into thine heart and knowledge is pleasant unto thy soul; Discretion shall preserve thee, understanding shall keep thee: That thou mayest walk in the way of good men, and keep the paths of the righteous." Proverbs 2:10–11, 20

So, go ahead, give your life to a cause, or to someone who truly loves you, but be careful not to give it to the wrong cause.

_____

_____

_____

_____

_____

_____

# Seeing the Good

People have so much good in them and each person is different from the next. Even the ones we might call abusers or narcissists, there is something good in each of them.

"So God created man in his own image, in the image of God created he him; male and female created he them." Genesis 1:21

Then in verse 31 it says, "And God saw everything that he had made, and, behold, it was very good ..."

Some abusers have many good qualities. Some can do math like geniuses; they may even find errors lawyers and bankers make. Just one look at the form in front of them, and they spot a mistake. On the rare occasion that they borrow a quarter or dollar from their wife or husband, they return it the next day. They never forget. Some never forget a birthday or anniversary and bring lavish gifts for such occasions. Some are fixers and nothing in the house ever breaks down without it being fixed immediately. Maybe they are bulb experts and notice every bulb every day whether it is burned out or not. Maybe they never miss an appointment or forget to turn a calendar page. Their bills are paid on time, and they keep no one waiting. They can carry on conversation like a pro and talk on any topic. They may bring home movies to watch and even allow their spouse some spending money. They may go on holidays together like a loving couple. What could possibly be wrong in such a marriage? Many women would envy such a wife with a husband like this.

Abusers often are the strictest law keepers. Laws for themselves, and laws for their spouse and children. They have reason to pride themselves in their self-made efforts. They certainly are close to perfect in so many ways. If an evolutionist saw him he'd be proud. He was well evolved he would say, and he did it all himself, against all odds, he would confess.

Scripture also says, "man's own righteousness is as filthy rags." Isaiah 64:6. One's own righteousness leads to pride, jealousies, self-righteousness, and many other sins. Though one can appear almost perfect to the human eye, compassion, mercy and love can be completely missing even when all the ACTS seem righteous.

> *"Woe unto you, scribes and Pharisees, hypocrites! for ye pay tithe of mint and anise and cummin, and have omitted the weightier matters of the law, judgment, mercy, and faith: these ought ye to have done, and not to leave the other undone." Matthew 23:23*

The abusive controller can have many positive traits that become easy to overlook when the abuse takes place. What better way to show God's love than to forgive. God can help us. Christ died for us while we were yet sinners. He died for those who will never accept His love. We may not be able to live with an abusive person but God can help us forgive them and show a measure of mercy on them.

Rather than hate them, give them over to God. He died for the worst of sinners and He knows what to do with people we have trouble with.

Yet the Word of God says, "We all have sinned and come short of the glory of God." Romans 3:23

# Are You Alive?

"The dead praise not the Lord ..."
Psalm 117:15

A sign of life is when you see growth and change. What kind of soil do you grow best in? As one can imagine, growth of any kind needs tending and care. A plant that is properly fed and watered does a lot better than one that is neglected. Sunshine and warmth is necessary for a plant's good health. Keeping out weeds is important, and keeping away the animals that would trample on the plant, as well.

Relationships work this way too. We all have somewhat different needs but on a general level, there are basic needs that we all have.

Who can thrive and grow when we put ourselves down? If an abusive person continually criticizes, it becomes easy to believe what they say, and then when they are not around, we continue this negative process. To feel you are not good enough, that you are not like the neighbors' wife or husband, that your mind is too stupid to grow and learn, that, should you have the chance to bloom, your flowers wouldn't be pretty anyway. These are terrible weeds that choke out any form of life and growth in you.

Those with a green thumb know how to nourish and care even for a sickly plant. They know the type of soil this plant would grow best in. What conditions it needs to revive. What the healthy plant looks like. They don't expect a daisy to look like a rose or vice versa. That would be crazy.

God is the best kind of gardener. He not only chose the different plants in His garden, He invented the idea of gardening and created the seed just the way He wanted it. Don't feel shy to go to Him and ask Him what kind of plant, (or person) you were meant to be. Then ask Him a favor. Ask Him to help you to keep the pesky weeds out. Learn to recognize the weeds. What to do with each kind. What are the friendly plants that grow beautifully alongside you?

Isaiah 42:3 says, "If you have been bruised, (abused) God will not discard of you. A bruised reed he will not break." ... If you are a smoldering wick, just a spark left in you, "and a smoldering wick he will not snuff out. In faithfulness he will bring forth justice."

God would have you healthy, vivacious, and fully alive so all will see His goodness and praise Him.

_____

_____

_____

_____

_____

_____

_____

_____

_____

# Making a Way Where There is No Way

For some people, there has to be a way, where there is no way.

Victims of abuse often feel very weak and think they must not be very smart. This is not the case. They may be paralyzed by fear but weak they are not, and incompetent they are not!

These victims of abuse need to know how to think around corners, in layers, covering all the what if's and what for's and how will you handle any surprise situation when bad gets worse. When all seems to have settled is often when the snake strikes. They learn to make a way around, through, under, over, any which way. They learn to peddle like a madman under water while holding everything together above water, calmly. They are kept so busy by the abuser that they don't even have time to give themselves credit where credit is due. Even thinking of taking credit can be to one's own detriment. Seeing confidence is a threat to the abuser, and if he or she sees a speck of confidence accidentally showing on one's face, they will start to tear you down.

Katie writes: "Only after I left the situation and looking back I could see how I did what normally would seem impossible. Day after day, year after year, I lived under severe pressure, not allowing myself to breathe or even think. Not allowing myself to grow wings or try out some dream. Believing the lie that I had no ideas. Believing the lie that I was a bump on a log, deader than a door nail, that I had no brain. I longed to prove it all wrong but I wasn't at all sure that it was wrong. That is, until I was set free."

"Once after we were already split," Kate continues, "the snake smirked and told me that he always knew that I was smart. That I would manage under any difficulties. It took a lifetime of years and me leaving, to tell me that! I have breathed the fresh air of freedom, experienced real love and acceptance, and now I give God all the credit for my survival and the rescue."

Kate writes, "Now in my present life, I am applying what I have learned in the tough times." Now she says, "Miraculously, God has made a way where there appeared to be no way."

_____

_____

_____

_____

_____

_____

_____

_____

_____

# Hope

"Hope deferred maketh the heart sick."
Proverbs 13:12

Hope is one of the most wonderful things in the whole world. It is like opening a door; like seeing out the window. It says you are not stuck. There is a way where there seemed not to be a way. Where there is hope there will be endurance, even in difficult times.

No one knows this better than a controlling person. They may make your life a living hell, but then they give you hope.

When you've had a rainy season you are so much more appreciative when the sun comes back out. After a harsh winter, one is gloriously happy when the snow melts and those little streams start flowing. Oh, we think we are in bliss! Who isn't more thankful for healing and good health than one who has just been through pain and suffering. When you feel the healing begin and you start getting back your strength, so also the hope rises. Soon you start planning projects to do and maybe places to go. When you finally get a breakthrough on your weight loss program, suddenly it becomes easier to stay away from the fatty foods and the sugars. Where before, it was like torture to stay out of the kitchen and the fridge, now suddenly it is not hard at all. Hope empowers and makes the tough jobs suddenly much easier.

Abusers are good listeners and watchers and know exactly what things are important to their gambit. Giving certain doses of hope to the victim is a big part of the game. Because they have stealthily studied you, they know just what amount of hope to give you in order for you to hang around to serve them and whatever their particular needs are. Then to make you dependent on them they also withhold what you desire the most.

**Taking care of yourself is always the number one priority if you live with an abuser.**

Hope is a most wonderful thing and will give you motivation to do things you wouldn't think you could ever do. Yet while with an abuser one needs to practice much wisdom and alertness. Know when this hope is false and only a game. Don't let yourself be manipulated, but as soon as you see such a practice going on make sure you are thinking for yourself and not following the cues of the manipulator. If it has been going on for any length of time you might need to escape to get your bearings back. Use every inch of strength you have to build up your self-esteem. Taking care of yourself is always the number one priority if you live with an abuser.

The very opposite is what the controllers wishes, so it will not be easy to stand your ground. When you see hope fade, run for help and Pray! There is strength available in the Lord, even for the weakest person. Your very breath can be a prayer. There are many verses in the Psalms that comfort and give strength.

Psalm 120:1 says, "In my distress I cried unto the Lord, and he heard me." As you read the scriptures, your faith and your strength will grow. The wisdom of God's Word will show you where true Hope lies.

# A Cripple

Though David was a king and lived in a palace, he was not too proud to take a cripple into his palace to live with him and dine with him at his very own table. "King David found Mephibosheth, Jonathan's crippled son, and brought him into his palace, and from then on, he ate at the King's table continually." Paraphrased from 2 Samuel 9:1–13

Mephibosheth was the disabled son of David's good friend Jonathan, and David remembered him some time after Jonathan had died in battle. "And Jonathan, Saul's son, had a son that was lame of his feet. He was five years old when the tidings came of Saul and Jonathan out of Jezreel and his nurse took him up, and fled; and it came to pass, as she made haste to flee, that he fell, and became lame. And his name was Mephibosheth." 2 Samuel 4:4

When King David remembered Mephibosheth and called for him to come to him and live in the palace. Mephibosheth's response to David's kindness was: "And he bowed himself, and said, What is thy servant, that thou shouldest look upon such a dead dog as I am?" 2 Samuel 9:8

In a sense, some of us have been disabled too, due to living with mental and emotional strain under the demands of an abuser. We may have lost our voice, our feelings, and our emotions as we try to deal with constant conflict in our home. Even with great efforts, we cannot put into words what is the matter. We may be too afraid to try. We may even feel like a 'dead dog', as Mephibosheth did.

As you have shut your mouth, you may have shut your brain down too. You don't know that you could survive on your own; that you could actually find your way through this entanglement if you were set free. You fear that if you opened your mouth, only screams might come out. You could fall apart and go completely crazy if you did open up.

You may be so 'crippled' by now that you cannot pick up a book and make sense of it; a book that some say would help you. Any advice given would not be heard because your mind is so uptight and only focused on the abuser. That fear has actually paralyzed you mentally.

Picture for a minute that King David comes along and wants you to come for dinner. Better yet, he sees your plight and wants you to move into his palace, and he himself will befriend you and speak confidence into your life. Every day you are welcome to eat at his table; to eat all the most rich and delicious foods available to a king. Picture dressing up in royal clothing. Picture discussing important topics with the king, and he is actually interested in what you have to say. He validates every little effort you make to express your thoughts, even your minutest ideas. Eventually, as you gain strength to dream again and to take small steps to carry out those dreams, he encourages you. Don't you think you would grow into confidence and soon you would be a different person?

**You are not what your abuser tells you that you are.**

You are not what your abuser tells you that you are. You don't deserve to do their work and yours as well, which never seems to end and bears no thanks.

Maybe you can't do anything about your situation today but you *can* begin to change your thinking. You can make a promise to yourself that no matter how things look outwardly you will begin to feel like a king's son or daughter on the inside. It need not be just a far-fetched daydream. You *are* a prince or princess in the sight of God.

The going might be slow but in time you will see more clearly. It will become more obvious to yourself that you are more capable than you ever imagined.

You have been staying strong in a very difficult place in your life. This is no small thing and few in this world manage that, with head held high. In time, God will give you your wings and you will fly. Maybe he will change your situation or you might leave the entanglement. In either case, you cannot lose when you are a child of the King.

_____

_____

_____

_____

_____

_____

_____

_____

_____

## Who is the Crazy One?

It is not only once that I've heard one call the abusing person crazy. They certainly don't appear that way when you meet them on the street and talk with them. Yet over and over they are being called crazy by those living with them.

Something very unusual about an abuser is that they have a certain kind of confidence in their wrongdoing. Their wrong can look so right you wonder who is the crazy one. Just the fact that they can stand up straight and look you right in the eye when they give crazy opinions and orders and explain it all in detail to look like it makes perfect sense, seems very odd. How gullible are we humans anyway that we can't figure them out and confront them openly? It always seems so elusive. We sense something wrong but can't tell exactly what it is. We laugh with them and talk with them, and even agree with them. *What can be so wrong?* we wonder. Almost like a blind person who feels their way around and can't quite make out what they are touching.

How did Hitler brainwash big strong German soldiers to kill Jews, just because of their religion? Can it get any crazier? The Jewish people were forced to wear bands around their arms so they could be identified easily. They couldn't share the same sidewalk with other people. Black people had the same problem in America. How can we, an educated and an intelligent people, stoop so low? The same question is often asked of victims of abuse. Why did you stay with such a person who tortures and abuses you every day? It's becoming the norm right under our noses to let people into our country who have a history of raping and killing, but I think therein lies the answer. It's because we are nice, and some of them are nice, so we simply can't say NO! We don't want to offend anyone.

It is very good and honorable and wonderful that we don't want to offend. We can all believe whatever we want and let everyone believe as they wish. This is how our country got to be a place of freedom and safety, with some exceptions.

Live and let live we say. We want to be peace lovers. We want to behave in such a way as we want others to do unto us. These are very good traits. Live with integrity. Isn't this the most Christian way to be? Save the planet. Work hard. Believe the best of everyone around us. This is Christianity at its best. If we would just all be kind and generous and eat healthy and soon we would achieve the 'lion lying down with the lamb' concept. We want to reach out to our neighbor and be the first to do so. Yet ... these are traits that can make us blind. We want to think the best of people, and we hope they do the same for us.

This creates a very big dilemma when we are with an abuser.

Don't push away your kindly traits just yet. They are good but that is not everything. A tiny bit of caution and mistrust never hurt anyone, not even the Christian. The Bible calls it discernment or wisdom. Even Jesus tested the waters sometimes to see where people were really at. You will feel a lot less crazy if you throw out a question now and then to keep yourself correctly informed.

Psalm 111:10 says, "The fear of the Lord is the beginning of wisdom; all who practice it have a good understanding. His praise endures forever!"

_____

_____

## Powerlessness

Is it true that if one musters up enough courage and strength one can overcome any obstacle? If you study hard enough, work hard enough any problem can be conquered? As young adults fresh out of high school or college are told, "You can be anything you want to be, if you want it badly enough."

Without discouraging hard work and determination there are some things in life not even blood sweat and tears can overcome. There are problems the most brilliant can't solve. A new belief is that we can talk about our problems or beliefs but we don't know anything for sure. Brilliant scholars say it is all debatable. It's all about talking a lot and knowing nothing for sure. Maybe we are all becoming something really fabulous but we don't know what it is. Such foggy thinking has never helped anyone overcome drug addiction or solved our society's problems of domestic abuse or fed the over twelve percent of the world that go hungry.

While governments legalize drugs and abortions there are people who have such monumental personal problems that they have lost all hope in ever having a normal life. There are the young people that have stood by when friends, victims of drug abuse, die of an overdose. How do they cope after such experiences? Some may become numb and hardhearted. Can we blame them? Some in hopelessness go deeper into drug abuse and crime. The silent pain that mothers of aborted babies carry is unbearable. The shame and despair they feel causes many disorders.

Alcoholics Anonymous teaches how important it is to admit powerlessness. That a Power greater than ourselves is the only way to recovery. Even the person who is being controlled by an abuser has to admit they are in deep trouble, helpless, and that they can't change their situation. Once realizing our powerlessness we stop the goose chase of self-assurance and start looking for help.

Countless times in the Bible David faces a difficult situation. Recorded over and over are the words, "and David inquired of the Lord." One such verse is found in 1 Chronicles 14:14. "David inquired again of God, and God said to him ..."

_____

_____

_____

_____

_____

_____

_____

_____

_____

## *Open My Eyes*

Elisha and the young man were in trouble but Elisha saw the army of angels who had come to protect them and fight for them. He prayed this prayer for the young man:

And Elisha prayed, and said, LORD, I pray thee, open his eyes, that he may see. And the LORD opened the eyes of the young man; and he saw: and, behold, the mountain was full of horses and chariots of fire round about Elisha. 2 Kings 6:17

When we are in trouble who do we trust to help us? Who will have our best interest in mind when we need it the most?

A trusting child is much easier to raise than one who likes to question everything you as a parent request of them. But a trusting person can get themselves into just as much, or maybe more, trouble than those who question everything.

If you are one of those wonderful trusting people who make the best of friends, you may need to pray that God opens your eyes to the possibility of trouble. Maybe you need to pray God open your eyes to the trouble you are already in. Sometimes, these wonderful trusting people will go year after year just trying to please a difficult spouse and always taking the blame for all the troubles. Sometimes, they wonder how they got into such a mess or sometimes they will have a meltdown and then they'll feel guilty for acting so foolishly. After a bad incident there is more submissive behavior to a spouse who uses and abuses them day after day. It just isn't in the hearts of some of these 'nice' people to ever raise a stink. "I'll try harder" is their motto. This is a wonderful trait when in a regular marriage but if you are being used, abused, and controlled it is time you wake up. A truly controlling person will be ruthless about all their multimillion dollar demands of you and think nothing of it.

**Of all personalities, the peace-loving person finds it most difficult to put up resistance.**

It will cost you to put on the brakes so be prepared. You are caught between a rock and a hard place. Of all personalities, the peace-loving person finds it most difficult to put up resistance. But if you don't, the abuser will chew you up and spit you out. An abuser needs a daily dose of "NO's" to all their ridiculous requests. With every NO you say you will become a little stronger.

Maybe you can do it for a time but it will wear you down to nothing, eventually. Controllers are the most difficult people to live with as they can be most stubborn but it's a setup. A setup so your fall will be more severe. Yes, it is wickedness what they do.

Cry out to the Lord to help you. As in Elijah's case, you will need angels and chariots of fire to help you. God did it for Elisha; He will do it for you too.

_____

_____

_____

_____

_____

## Lying Vanities

"They that observe lying vanities forsake their own mercy."
Jonah 2:8

Pretending can be fun for a child and adults make careers out of acting. There are jokers that love fooling people for a good laugh. At what point does acting become lying and cruel?

Some have questioned whether faith is just lying to yourself and putting on a good act, until you actually fall for your own lies.

We are born with a certain amount of faith and even the atheist believes in things he can't see or prove. "...faith is the substance of things hoped for, the evidence of things not seen." Hebrews 11:1.

Pretending and acting come so easy to us humans. Most of us like to make good impressions and sometimes even fool ourselves into thinking we are better than what we really are.

Some people are very good at keeping a straight face and showing no emotion. They might make good poker players. Some people think their face would break if they let you know what they really feel. Some keep a poker face for reasons of safety. Still it is hiding who you really are and what you really think.

Abusers and controllers are good at mind games. If they see what you like or what you don't like they will make sure they do the opposite around you. This is to make you uncomfortable and to catch you off guard. Around controllers, even a child learns quickly how to lie. Lying in order to get what you want and lying to keep out of trouble.

In the Garden of Eden, Adam and Eve covered their naked bodies, hiding from God. The Lord called to them after they had sinned, but they were ashamed of their nakedness. It's the uncovering that we are afraid of. There is much covering up going on these days.

It takes faith to disrobe what is on the inside of us. The enemy accuses – one day he tempts us to uncover and the next day he shames the nakedness. The Father God wants a true uncovering. For a true relationship with Him we must come humbly, without the covering of pride.

Before him we are naked because He sees through everything anyway.

In John 4, Jesus sees right into the life of the Samaritan woman. He knew she had had five husbands, and the current man she was living with was not her husband. She was not afraid of Jesus but was amazed and rejoiced greatly and ran into her town to tell everyone that she met the Messiah, the man who knew everything about her.

Jesus came to restore people and relationships. There is no need to cover up with false attitudes around Him. He wants us in Spirit and in Truth. In John 4:24 it says, "God is a Spirit and they that worship him must worship him in spirit and in truth."

The Spirit world is more real than this physical world. The Lord said, "This world will pass away and all the lusts therein. By His word His kingdom will be established forever."

If it weren't so tragic, it would be funny how people run to and fro here on the earth, running after styles, technology, more money, faster cars, a cleaner house, and in the olden days it was, who had more canning in their cellar pantry. People are running here there and everywhere, but what are they really accomplishing? The fast-paced city life is a fake. We were not meant to live like this and it often does damage to us mentally and physically.

Sometimes it takes a 'simple' person to see that we are in a fast lane chicken race. Have we become like chickens running around with their heads chopped off? They still move and splat around but they are dead on the inside.

Many of those who are tired of the rat race choose to go back to the country. They want what's real and long for what is close to the heart; becoming more self sufficient and not so dependent on technology. There are just certain 'God things' that don't have to be explained to country people.

It might be those who live closer to the earth know better how to strip down and be real before God and one another. To walk and talk humbly with the Lord is the most real place to be.

Even in Jesus' day, there were people who would rather chase after the dos and don'ts, after Pharisaical law, than to be set free by the grace and love of the Lord Jesus.

They didn't appreciate the Lord Jesus because he told them the truth. They killed Him, but he came back to life. He went back to heaven but sent the Holy Spirit to the disciples and Christians, and now there were many preaching the true gospel. He is still the truth and the life, the way to God; and He loves us, and will take us just as we are, like the Samaritan woman at the well who rejoiced at hearing the truth.

## A Prie Dieu (Pre de you)

> "Come, let us worship and bow down,
> Let us kneel before the LORD our Maker."
> Psalm 95:6

Bowing down and kneeling are signs of humility. They are signs of submission, of being unpretentious, compliant, accepting someone's authority, as in bowing to a king.

Sometimes it is done in piety and for show; its sincerity is absent in such cases. Who then do we bow to? Would it be someone we trust? Also someone who is in authority?

God is someone who has ultimate authority and someone we can trust. He came humbly to earth, even humbly before mankind, though he was God. If God Almighty can be humble before us, mere man, how much more would it be our place to come humbly before Him, on bended knee?

He did more than bend his knees, washing his disciple's dirty feet. He died on a criminal's cross. It was completely unfair yet completely appropriate. After all, He took on Himself the sins of the whole world. And took our punishment for it. Yet He is so humble that we are not forced to take this great gift of sins forgiven; that he lets us chose to accept or reject Him.

There are those who may not know God at all but they still find someone or something to worship. Something to be obsessed about, spend all their time thinking about and talking about. It could be an author, movie star, or musician. Maybe it's eating and food. On the other hand, it could be keeping a perfect body and exercising. Maybe for some it is learning and obsessions with education. Maybe, whom to marry and having children. Some people are obsessed with their religion, however they see it, not necessarily fitting with scripture.

There are people who obsess over their spouse or children. They want complete control of them and hold on to them as if they own them. There is co-dependency where people hold on to each other and with that come all kinds of expectations of each person in order to hold up the needy relationship.

In rare cases, a parent attaches themselves so tightly to their adult child that the grown offspring can never leave home. They may plead helplessness when the child wants to move out, or say outrageous things like, "God told me that you should stay home and take care of me." Thus they cruelly stunt the growth of their offspring to the point of disabling them. What could be more cruel?

A victim of abuse also obsesses. They obsesses over being completely obedient to the perpetrator of abuse in order to avoid violence. They can think of nothing else. Such obsessions are like worship and is extremely detrimental to one's mental and physical well-being.

Therefore, always be careful who you revere and especially whom you worship. "And Jesus answered and said unto him ... for it is written, Thou shalt worship the Lord thy God, and Him only shalt thou serve. Luke 4:8 KJV

No need for a prie dieu to kneel on for your worship. Just bend your knee wherever you are; and if your heart is humble before the Maker of heaven and earth; He will hear you. If you listen closely you will hear from heaven, many things that will help you. Help you out of a controlling situation and also keep you from being that overpowering individual.

# A Normal Day in an Abnormal Life

Alarm rings, Sheila gets up. Depressed but no time for it. Children all grown up and moved out; thank God for that! Most mothers ached for her children as they left the nest, but not Sheila, she was glad they were out from under their roof of their criminally controlling father. But now there was no time to think. Not of her children nor of herself. There was only time for HIM. He sucked up any life she still had in her and then when that was gone, she had none left for anything else.

Sheila knows, as she puts her feet on the floor that she will fail today but that can't stop her. It's time to start coffee and make a quick lunch for the man she is living with and calls her husband. He hurts her with words, and her thoughts are consumed with how she will answer to this or that. Her brain automatically scans all his needs and demands. Socks in the drawers, table clear. Oh Lord let there be a bran muffin still in the freezer, Oh, Lord, the clothes in the dryer, run and get those pants. If they aren't in the closet by the time he gets up there will be a debate and then the interrogation will never end.

She never had any right answers for him that would satisfy. Thank God, they are in the dryer, and she brings them upstairs and hangs them in the closet. Glancing at the time, she knows to wake him now.

Yes, he has an alarm clock but it would be too much to ask him to get up on his own. Running to the bathroom to make sure there's a clean towel, and they must hang even. She grabs the old ones and wipes the sink, toilet and floor with it. Oh, and she reaches to the top of the door frame and gives that a quick wipe with a smirk. "Now, finally, I'm a step ahead of HIM. Everything shines and that is all that matters."

Back she goes to the kitchen to be completely alert and happy now. "Good morning!" she greets the expressionless face now in the kitchen. There is no answer. Only, "Where's the coffee?", when it's not instantly forthcoming. Chipper, she pours it and quickly sits down to pray, "Thank you Lord for this food, I pray that you will bless it to our bodies. Amen."

On this day she opens the Daily Bread Devotional and reads. They eat their muffin with their coffee. She busies herself waiting for him to leave for work. The ritualistic dry kiss and fake calm smile must come first before he can be gone. "Have a good day now."

He shuts the door behind him and she hears the truck start up. She is free to do whatever she wants for about ten hours but finds she has no ambition. She wanted to do all sorts of things, but now she wants to do nothing. So she goes into eating mode and writing mode and doing nothing mode. She feels horrible but she has no energy or ambition to do what she should be doing. Not even for what she wanted do to. The hours roll by. Every inch of work she does seems like pushing a cart of rocks uphill. She has no interest in any of her work. The guilt is laying heavy, and the unworthiness, but she has no ambition.

Little by little she gets some things done. This until about an hour or so before that face reappears in the doorway, gray, with deep-set eyes and a well-carved frown. Suddenly, she is motivated to think and to rush around the house. Oh, my god, what will she cook for supper? Did she do all he demanded and would be expecting? Is the table clear? Are the curtains straight?

Does the chair touch the rail? The garden, the basement, the mail, did she forget to go and get it, is the shower curtain fixed? Scan, scan, hurry, hurry, guilt, supper, act naturally, smile, poker face smile, chin up, rehearsing what to say if he is angry, calmly.

This seems to be the only thing she is good at, knowing how to rush about and anticipate HIS thousands of demands. Even so, she never got it all right. She'll have to learn to say sorry quicker, she thinks. But she knows she will not – because she's not to blame. It never comes out sincere, and it wouldn't help anyway.

This day, he looks around and frowns when he comes in the door. It must be a good day because all he can do is mutter under his breath and then walk off to the computer to busy himself. I guess some days are better than others, she thinks, hopefully it will stay this way till bedtime.

## Another Victim's Life

He prepared the turkey the night before Thanksgiving Day. Potatoes were peeled and all the vegetables ready to go for the morning. All the prep work done as was clearly instructed him by his very particular wife.

When he and his wife met he knew she was a very determined woman, but he loved such a strong woman, who spoke her mind. She certainly would be a help to him as he would need to focus on his grain farm for a living. She would keep him grounded is what he thought. The land was rich and grains grew abundantly. It meant a lot of hours each day of work but he was young and energetic; he could easily provide for a family; the family he would have.

He had time for hockey with friends on outdoor hockey rinks in the winter time and worked the fields all summer. It was a great life. He was tall, lean, muscular and a very friendly chap.

Now he was ready for marriage and up for this exciting challenge. She was a great cook even at a young age. She had no trouble telling him what to do and even on their wedding day her instructions to him were heard across the room. People thought it was rather adoring how this most handsome young man followed his bride, all decked in white lace, blond curls falling on her shoulders, giving the appearance of an angel; how he followed her every cue, as she wagged her pretty pink finger at him.

It started on their honeymoon though, when he realized that this would not be a marriage made in heaven. Nothing was as he had expected and as she had promised, and it never would be. She made him run errands, get rid of all his hobbies and throw out the skates, his music and any dream he might have had. She wanted to go to town and shop, do coffee with friends, gossip on the phone for hours.

He gave up the farm he so loved to work in the city. Then when he came home he did all the cooking and cleaning and taking care of the children. She always had some important business to attend to that took her out of the house into her social circles.

Thus their lives were lived. He became an empty shell living for a wife that lived for a purposeless, yet driven life.

When she took sick with heart problems, she again, was the center of attention. He had to run after all her complaints and demands. At church, he would sit alone while she made her social rounds and every Sunday took the pastor's time with all her ailments.

One day, this poor man was found dead, never having lived.

# A Broken World

We live in a broken world. This mess started in the Garden of Eden and mankind has either tried to fix it in their own strength, or kept breaking it more.

This is why we need grace and forgiveness every day. We need God to help us make sense of it and show us how to walk in it. The good can look bad and the bad good. It doesn't help to judge others because if we look a little closer, we will see what is not so good in ourselves.

Some people love to try to keep the law and work at it feverishly day and night. They may even make themselves sick in trying to keep all the rules. They keep their own laws and then make others around them keep them also. It is so much work it takes up their every waking hour. If only everyone worked as hard as they did then this world would be fixed and run smoothly and be a wonderful place for all to live in.

Other people are more carefree. Some may even call them irresponsible. They believe that if they do the bare minimum, mind their own business and enjoy life in a somewhat chaotic state, all will be well. If we all did this, this world would be a perfectly happy place to live in.

Whether one fits in either of these groups or somewhere in between, we never will hit the mark perfectly. So then, we might ask as the disciples did in John 6:28-29: "Then said they unto him, what shall we do, that we might work the works of God? Jesus answered and said unto them, this is the work of God, that ye believe on him whom he hath sent."

We may judge ourselves harshly but God has a better way. 'Trust Him', as He has already planned a way for us to live peacefully and harmoniously with each other and with Him.

Believe! That is our work. Believe in the work of the cross; for our freedom and forgiveness, for our healing whether it's body, mind, or spirit. Believe He is an ever present help in trouble. Believe that He can make our crooked paths straight.

Believe in that still small voice of The Almighty. "And thine ears shall hear a word behind thee, saying, This is the way, walk ye in it, when ye turn to the right hand, and when ye turn to the left." Isaiah 30:21

We may need to wait for God to fix this world, but we can walk through it in freedom.

# *Warnings*

"Don't walk too close to the cliff!" "Put your coat on before going out into the cold." "You eat that, it will kill you." "Keep driving like that, there will be an accident..." "If you marry that man or woman, you will pay for it."

Warning signs can be read everywhere and yet we get ourselves into predicaments. We may do everything possible to proceed with caution but there seem to be unforeseen objects just waiting to trip us up.

John 10:10 says, "The thief cometh not, but for to steal, and to kill, and to destroy."

But Jesus came to give us life, and that ... abundantly!"

Abusers can drive you so hard and if you get caught up in the frazzling madness, you sometimes become like puppets that just keep going even when they are ready to give out or collapse.

**When you are over your head in trouble – STOP! Stop all your fighting and struggling. Admit you can't do it.**

When you have done all and the buzzing never stops. When you are over your head in trouble – STOP! Stop all your fighting and struggling. Admit you can't do it. Instead of wasting yourself till the death – give up!

We are so programmed to fight to the finish but some fights are not worth it. They will finish you before you finish the fight. Those are the times to give up early on. Go on strike, stay in bed, don't do anything. Maybe you need to be drastic about it. Don't go to work. Yes, quit your job. No notice, nothing! Pack your bags and leave town. Drive even though you don't know where you're going. Take your kids to your mother's and tell her you'll be back in a couple of days. Take the time to figure out what you can do. You are doing a terrible thing but a terrible problem needs a terrible solution.

Some types of suffering are honorable but suffering from the hands of an abuser is only destruction. It destroys yourself and harms your children. There is no honor in suffering when you are stuck with someone who doesn't let up. Where is the praise to God in that?

You are in a place where any and every choice you need to make is difficult. Your road has not been for the faint, and even as you make big decisions, you will get the strength. You feel weak but you are much stronger than most people. Anyone who has lived with an abuser knows that you have to have the strength of a mountain lion just to survive.

As you stop all, cry to the Lord to help you to make some life-changing decisions. Don't give up even as you might run into trouble. Sometimes you might have to backtrack some but have it in mind to find relief. Treat it like a race you are set on winning. With determination, faith in God and some help from real friends, you will get out of your troubles and be free again.

_____

_____

_____

_____

# Be a VICTOR

A victor is the opposite of a victim. Sometimes we are victims and there is nothing we can do about it at the time. It takes strength and courage to become a victor in victim situations.

A victim is a person harmed, injured, or even killed as a result of a crime, accident, or other event or action.

On the other hand, victim mentality is an acquired (learned) personality trait in which a person tends to regard him or herself as a victim.

A person can pretend to be a victim to get what they want in life. They might pretend to be sick so people will feel sorry for them and come and visit. They may complain of poverty so friends will give them money. They may make excuses that sound like reasons and even work up real tears to get out of doing what they don't want to do.

A victim of domestic control and violence is not like that but is a true victim. They must always be taken seriously whatever it is they say. Often, it takes every ounce of strength they have to tell someone even a small portion of what they are experiencing.

Although these victims of violence are often the strongest most kind, loving, and Godly people, there might linger with them a victimhood that they can't shake. They may work feverishly at shedding the victim syndrome but they need a little help to become even stronger and wiser to the abuser and more confident in their dealings with the controller.

## There may be good times, good moments, good days – build on these.

If you choose to stay with the abuser for your own honorable reasons it would be important to become an expert at becoming and staying strong. Focus on what you CAN control. Count your blessings, even the very small ones. Be as creative as you can in managing the abuse. Ignore the negative as much as possible and give yourself all the credits you possibly can for keeping the relationship together. It is not selfish but life preserving. There may be good times, good moments, good days – build on these. Then do not let the memory of the horrible days eat up the happy moments. Know where it all comes from and move forward.

Make it your goal to be proactive, to keep the peace in the midst of a type of war zone; to be an overcomer when all the chips are down; to take charge even when you feel powerless.

There are some who would say this is impossible but Ephesians 6:10–12 has the answer: "Finally, my brethren, be strong in the Lord, and in the power of His might. Put on the whole armour of God, that ye may be able to stand against the wiles of the devil. For we wrestle not against flesh and blood, but against principalities against powers, against the rulers of the darkness of this world, against spiritual wickedness in high places."

_____

_____

_____

_____

_____

## Standing Strong

Has it been hard to stand strong in the face of your abuser? Have you felt like a wimp with no backbone? You are much stronger than you think.

Abusers are the most difficult people to stand up to because they have ways; unsuspecting ways, that are impossible to figure out. Sometimes the abuse becomes so forceful if it were a wind storm it would be a Category 5 hurricane. Sometimes the abuse comes as unsuspecting as a snake slithering through the grass.

If you are planning to leave your abuser, you must reach deep inside of you to the strength that you possess. You have survived abuse, you certainly will survive leaving the abuser.

You cannot waiver because that is the place where the rope is weakest. Emotions come and go and zig zag and flop around like a spineless guppy fish. When you make the decision, stick with it. Depression and loneliness can be overcome. Becoming depressed is no fun at all, but you can get out of it if you work at good self-talk or if you go for counselling and to support groups. If you lean on people heavily for a while that is okay. You will get over it and become strong in time. Insecurity and fear can end up in power and fearlessness. Going back to your abuser will only make you weaker and more unsure.

If you fumble and stumble for a while, know that is normal. If you feel like you cannot trust your own mind, that is a normal feeling. If you feel you are going crazy, that is also normal in your situation.

There is no need to put yourself down for that. This is very new to you and it will be weird but if you find someone to talk to and a support group, you will soon have clear direction.

You may never have stood your ground in the face of your abuser, but if you decide to leave the caustic relationship you need to show them you are truly serious. Just use the same strength that helped you survive abuse, to stand your ground and survive the changes after leaving the abuser.

Know that you are smart and strong. If you are not, then there is help out there for you. Going back to your abuser is only going to make you weak and unsure. If you fumble and stumble for a while, know that is normal. If you feel like you cannot trust your own mind that is a normal feeling.

**Remember, you have been lied to about your capabilities so believe that you can, and you will do it.**

You need some money to start with and a place to put your head and a bit of time. Someone who can give you positive support in the early days of separation is greatly helpful. Give yourself a bit of time and you will soon find your feet and will learn much faster than you ever imagined. Remember, you have been lied to about your capabilities so believe that you can, and you will do it.

In all your years of abuse you likely learned to pray very well. When you are alone and lonely keep on praying like you always did. If you don't know how then this is a perfect time to learn. It is not so much about the technique but the sincerity. God has many wonderful surprises waiting for you, and you will smile again, and you will laugh and have a peace that passes all comprehension.

> *"Trust in the LORD with all thine heart; and lean not unto thine own understanding. In all thy ways acknowledge him, and he shall direct thy paths." Proverbs 3:5–6*

There is temporary help for your loneliness till you find your direction and purpose. Here are a few examples. You can make your own list of what helps you.

- Get in the car and go for a drive.
- Go to public places like the mall, or to church, or to a library; somewhere where there are people.
- Go for nature walks in safe places, where there are houses around and other people walking.
- Stay away from people who hurt you or make you feel bad.
- Do what you enjoy: read, write, watch movies, do puzzles, play music, stay up all night, sleep in.
- Buy yourself a treat; be it favorite foods, or a new pair of shoes, or maybe a beautiful plant or a small candle.
- Change something about yourself like hairdos or a new style of clothes, or learning something you never thought you would do.
- Buy a pass to the gym or to a public pool, and maybe take swimming lessons.
- Visit the elderly at a nursing homes or the sick at the hospital. It will help you in your loneliness as you also help someone else.
- Take up painting, carving, fishing, carpentry ... knitting ... whatever you feel is most therapeutic. Don't wait till you are good at it. This is the time to try something new.
- Go to church, join clubs, take some classes. You will soon have a small group of friends, and you will realize you are becoming more comfortable all the time with yourself.
- Give yourself positive self-talk whenever you think of it.

- Begin a habit of thankfulness. Count your blessings and thank God for each one. They are sure to multiply and soon you will have a thankful spirit about you.
- Read and fall in love with the Word of God. Don't make a religion out of it, just read over and over what helps you most and God will open many more scriptures to your heart. Soon you will be completely amazed at what all He has for you to learn and enjoy. He never runs out and you will never get bored.

## *"And it Came to Pass ..."*

The Bible has many scriptures with the words, '...and it came to pass.' When something has come to pass then something must have passed and is gone. (Old has passed, new has come.) Here is one woman's story of 'it came to pass.'

Tracy married a young handsome man, had four lovely children, but he did not treat her right. Even while she was a young blushing bride this man created fear and dread in his bride. The mixture of torment and an appearance of love, was cause for great confusion.

Her children watched as their mother got physically beaten and mentally put down. She did her best in a crippled kind of way, but she had been brainwashed into thinking she was not a capable mother.

As her brain got twisted into knots of lies mixed with negativity, she did everything to fight for her sanity. Even at her lowest points she found bits of time for reading, learning, thinking, journaling, as well as reading the scriptures and praying when she could. Little by little these things gave her strength. She kept all this to herself. It was a very lonely survival.

But it came to pass that the old life ended, and a new life began. It took till half her life had passed but a new life did eventually come to be.

All her years of experience took her through many stages of learning. She went from shock and despair, to searching and reading, to finding answers and becoming less afraid. She became desperate to know God and pounded her prayers out on her walking trails. The more she studied the scriptures the more answers she found and the more hungry she became to know more.

Even while her grown children were helping her to freedom, something in her mind began to change. It suddenly opened, and she began to learn normal life skills rather than just what she was instructed and demanded to learn.

Old things had passed, and behold all things had become new.

The years of torment had ended and it was a new day on the Earth for this woman.

God is a God of new beginnings. When His Son Jesus died on the cross, it brought hope to all mankind for forgiveness of sin. Not a beginning of more rules and laws but a beginning of freedom in Christ

# Are We Hearing Right?

*"Let favor be shewed to the wicked, yet will he not learn
righteousness: in the land of uprightness will he deal unjustly, and
will not behold the majesty of the LORD."*
Isaiah 26:10

Jesus, the blameless and righteous One, preached and showed love
and mercy for three years while He was on earth and yet many did
not appreciate His goodness and eventually had Him killed. As Jesus
was being tried Pilate said about Him ...

"Pilate saith unto him, What is truth? And when he had said this,
he went out again unto the Jews, and saith unto them, I find in him no
fault at all." John 18:38

Yet, Pilate listened to the pressure of the people that were shouting for Him to be killed. Just as Pilate did, victims of abuse often
cave in under the pressure of their abuser. They go against all their
better judgments and cater to the controller's shouts and dictates
and pressures.

On one hand we know that as Christians it is a good thing to love
your enemies and bless those that curse you. On the other hand,
abusers take your love and stamp it in the dirt. Some even take the
Word of God and preach it to you according to their twisted ears,
completely losing the essence of what is said. We assume abusers
have it wrong but what about victims of abuse?

How can you be sure, as a victim of abuse, that you are right in the way you do good? You may be catering to the abuser out of fear, and think that your 'nice' is God's will. Is it nice to encourage their bad behavior by running after their every demand? Would it really be God's will for you to cater to abusive ways and lies of the abuser?

Much is done in the name of good, but is it really good?

Our minds are capable of playing many games and tricks so question yourself. Are you being kind and loving in the right way to your abuser?

Don't just listen to your own frightened voice on what is right and wrong thing to do in your difficult situation. Ask God whether you've got it right? Ask for a long-term solution that will bring peace. Ask any questions you might have. Then listen carefully at what God shows you. God's imagination is ever greater than your own. It might surprise you what He will tell you as a solution.

> *"Call unto me, and I will answer thee, and shew thee great and mighty things, which thou knowest not."*
> *Jeremiah 33:3*

---

---

---

---

---

# Arise, Walk

> "Arise, walk through the land in the length of it and
> in the breadth of it; for I will give it unto thee.
> Then Abram removed his tent,
> and came and dwelt in the plain of Mamre,
> which is in Hebron, and built there an alter unto the Lord."
> Genesis 13:17–18

Going through life there will be landmarks that mark out important posts, meaningful lessons, significant truths learned and accomplishments to remember. Even as a very young person you might be able to see some of these markings already.

Life is not without meaning, though on a day to day basis, a young person might wonder, "Why am I here?" "Is there a map somewhere or a significant destination I am headed for that I might not know about?" "Is my destination what I decide it will be or is there a higher hand mapping out a specific target?" Maybe it is a bit of both, my decision plus a higher power doing the steering in my life.

Some things are out of one's control: who our parents are, what country we are born in, our personalities, or where in the family line you were born.

Most of us make decisions in our life that we feel best suit us. Then as life goes on we might wish in hindsight we had made different decisions.

If you have been caught in an abusive, even violent relationship, it is quite obvious you would not have chosen such a relationship had you known what you would encounter. The abuser is usually very good at courting their lover and convincing you of their deep love for you.

How can one distinguish between what is real love and what is a manipulator's love? The one with real love does not always come in a perfect wrap either. Sometimes, the manipulator comes in a more perfect package than the one who is genuine.

If you are a person who trusts easily then beware. A manipulator can sniff you out pretty quick and you are the one they will pursue. In any case, none of us plan to marry someone who will use and abuse us and who will control and manipulate us all the days of our lives. If you are in such a relationship, you are among the strongest most determined most faithful of all people. Your daily road is by far the most difficult.

You may feel you are to blame for your troubles. Wait just a minute. God has a plan for you even if you have sidestepped a better path or made a poor decision.

All through the Bible there are examples of people making mistakes, and God still had very important work for them to do once they committed their lives to Him. There is great potential, even for a wasted life, if put in the hands of God.

> *"Humble yourselves in the sight of the Lord, and He shall lift you up." James 4:10*

## Being a Valiant Soldier

When times are good, be happy,
but when times are bad, consider this:
God has made the one as well as the other.
Taken from Ecclesiastes 7:14.

Are you having a good day? Praise the Lord!

People who live in abusive situations do have good days. Their controlling partner might need a break from all their commotion and decide one day to be sweet and nice and even give you some freedom to go do whatever it is you want. Maybe they treat you wonderfully with your favorite meal or plan a holiday they want to go on with you. They might even come and snuggle with you and suggest you watch your favorite movie together with popcorn and treats and everything. You might talk and laugh together and soon you find yourself confiding some inside deep down thoughts and wishes that you have.

You are so sure that finally all your efforts are paying off and your marriage will finally be what you always knew it could be. You tell yourself that everyone has marriage problems and that is no reason to leave. Love is patient and kind and forgives, doesn't count up all the wrongs. You are not perfect either, you tell yourself, and it is only the right thing to do, to extend the long arm of forgiveness to your spouse whom you love. You fully understand that some marriages are more difficult than others and you have made up your mind to stay for the long haul. You may even have shut the door tight to consider leaving. You will do the nobler thing and not become another divorce statistic.

Definitely, some days are better than others, even when living with a difficult person. Maybe you are settling for the best possible in your situation. Maybe you think it is quite bearable and to leave the situation is absurd since you desire from the bottom of your heart for the family to stay together. That together with the hardship you would cause, should you leave, keeps you where you are, year after year. It would be such an upheaval to leave! On the good days you feel that the good still outweighs the bad. You have become tough. You have learned all the tricks and feel you are becoming quite good at the balancing act, which is your daily living and breathing and you might even be proud of what you have learned.

You're the Mama or Papa who can keep it all together and all under the covers. You may feel strongly that this is your place for now and that God will reward you someday. Be sure that he will!

**You must know that you are a heroic person. You are walking a more difficult road than most ...**

Having said this, you are to be respected for your bravery. You must know that you are a heroic person. You are walking a more difficult road than most and you are a valiant soldier. May the Lord God of heaven and earth walk closely with you and watch over you day and night. May He watch over your coming in and your going out and bless you in all your ways. May your decision to stay in such a marriage and show love the best you can, reap great benefits in the future. God Bless You.

## As a Man Thinks

What does a person think in his heart?

It is said that a person has three places where they think: in the brain, in the heart, and in the stomach. As the little story goes, "When I first saw the young man, I had a gut feeling he was bad news, and after letting him stay for a week I knew in my head that I should kick him out, but after seeing his remorse my heart told me to give him another chance."

In the Bible, David was a man after God's own heart. We all know we have sinned and David also, and displeased God in many occasions but his heart was always toward God.

It was not keeping all the laws that made David righteous in God's eyes, but it was a heart that loved God and His word. Psalm 18:1 says that he loved God's word and delighted in it. Psalm 119:103 states, "How sweet are thy words unto my taste! Yea, sweeter than honey to my mouth!"

An abuser may have you running in a vicious circle. One day they appear like they are good and kind and then the next day something sets them off and they are vicious monsters. They keep you hoping for something better but the chase doesn't end. They might even cry and say sorry for hitting you or maybe do a fake apology just for points, but their heart is not pure and true. Only God sees hearts, so go to Him on what to do with the situation.

Your heart may be well intentioned in staying with the abuser, while your gut tells you to go, and your head doesn't make sense of any of it. One day you think it's terrible of you to still stay living with this person and then when they let up their horrible actions you again hope that things will get better and improve. After all, divorce is such a huge step to take. The years can slip by like this and all that ever changes is that you become more used to the abuse and perhaps learn to outsmart the abuser now and then in his crooked ways.

Take a moment, or a day, to stop the chase and take inventory of your situation. You certainly have an abundance of strength or you wouldn't have survived such a tyrannical situation. Are you nursing a bad marriage and thus encouraging the bad behavior? Are there children involved who are getting hurt or learning the behavior of an abuser? Have you let yourself drown in all the troubles that you are in and now you can't even look after yourself, never mind the children?

Your heart may be in the right place but you have no strength to take any action. Although some people may not understand you or even churches who wouldn't be helpful, there is help out there if you dare to ask or have access to the Internet. Domestic abuse is kept very secret in many cases.

A good place to start is to talk to God about it and ask Him to open the right doors for you to find help. Even small steps in the right direction will eventually get you out of your bad situation.

# Don't Fold Your Hands

"But God hath chosen the foolish things
of the world to confound the wise;
and God hath chosen the weak things of the world to confound
the things which are mighty …"
1Corinthians 1:27

Don't fold your hands in hopelessness. Don't think, 'I can't', thoughts. Hurry to God's mercy seat to see what he has for you. Perhaps you could set up your own throne room where you pray and tell God everything.

It is not by our own earthly might and power that we hear God but it is by God's Spirit that we can hear Him speak. This does not mean that you can't think things with your own mind or read books and learn all sorts of things but there is so much more added to your own knowledge if you put God first and heed to His Words through His Spirit – the Holy Spirit. You don't have to wait to be highly educated to understand God's voice. He speaks to the simple as He speaks to anyone who would listen.

If you are in a very difficult situation; living with a person who harshly controls you and rules over you, telling you believable lies, don't just sit by and take it. If you are told that you could not manage without them; that you do everything wrong; you may be tempted to mentally fold your hands and give up trying to use your mind and worse yet, give up listening to God, the Holy Spirit.

There are several scriptures that might encourage you to turn your eyes back to God and expect to hear from Him once again.

> *"... O man greatly beloved, fear not: peace be unto thee, be strong, yea, be strong. And when he had spoken unto me, I was strengthened, and said, Let my lord speak; for thou hast strengthened me." Daniel 10:19*

Joe was in a difficult marriage where he was told when to come and when to go. He had a very kind heart and was not one who would talk down to any woman, but treated all women with gentleness and respect. Even though his heart was in much pain, he endured. He patiently took it all to the Lord. Circumstances finally led him out of this relationship but he became a pillar of stability in people's lives and a prayer warrior for those in need.

God cares about the 'one on one' relationships, as He cares about each individual person. He has chosen the weak things of the world to confound the mighty. Even when you are in a difficult place and you don't think you have anything strength left, take courage. He cares about each of us – one on one. "My strength is made perfect in weakness ..." 1 Corinthians 12:9

God can use the foolish things of this world to confound the wise, so lift up those hands that hand down and do what you can. God will strengthen you even in your weakness.

_____

_____

_____

## Be Creative

If you are in the middle of a very difficult marriage and you see no way out, try to be creative within the abusive situation. It will put a whole new spin on abuse and you will be motivated to take positive action, rather than continuously living under oppression, depression and hopelessness.

God can use the abuser's tactics for your good. For example, when the abuser preaches at you, even though it's legalistically, it can actually be helpful, if you interpret it correctly. Some lessons learned under heavy rule, can at another time in life, be quite beneficial.

There are many things one can learn while someone is breathing down your neck while you work, complaining over petty non issues, or instructing you on how to do everything. You could learn how to work hard and do your job perfectly. You could learn how to ignore distractions. You could learn not to be afraid of lions, tigers, or cobras. You could also learn how to answer wisely and creatively.

When you stop being afraid, all kinds of other doors open up to you. You can observe them meticulously. Not to get them back because that will never be to your benefit. But it will do you more good if you observe them closely. You will catch them in their own snares. You won't have to say much, just notice it and smile and wink at them when you see it happen. You can learn to smile. Quiet smiling can be very unnerving to a controller.

If your workload is unbearably heavy, then find secret ways to make shortcuts. This can be very useful craft at other times as well. If you are being watched every minute and you have no freedom; become creative in giving excuses for doing what you want to do. Use the things they allow you to do to include other activities alongside your allowed activity.

Still one of the wisest, smartest, most clever, brainy things to do when you live with someone who abuses you, is tell them as little as possible. Remember, yours is not a normal relationship and accept it for what it is. Don't expect anything different because only God knows how to deal with these people. You don't, I don't, and I don't know of anyone who does.

The Bible doesn't say that all things in life are easy but it does say that "ALL things work together for good to them that love God." It might be a good idea to – rather than run after the wind, after all the demands of the abusive party – put your ALL into the one who Wants to and would Love to help you, the Lord Jesus Christ.

You will become, wise and smart; you will be comforted in your troubles; you will find peace and love in your heart; you will even find an overwhelming measure of joy. The Bible says, that "the joy of the Lord is your strength" (Nehemiah 8:10b), so you will also gain strength to bear your burdens. At the right time, God will help you out of your situation. Try to learn as much as possible in the meantime.

_____

_____

_____

_____

_____

## Changes Can Be Scary

Even good changes can be scary. We like to know what will happen next, to give us a certain amount of control.

This is no different than when you are in an abusive situation. You have learned what to do when. You have learned to cope and then to hope. Sometimes there seem to be good times of reward for your efforts. That is, until the next blow up or surprise crash, in your good times. You have learned so many tricks, that playing tricks become fun in a sick kind of way, and you would almost miss the way you cope with a miserable situation. You lift yourself up in pride at how you have learned to outsmart the abuser. This is your life. This is familiar. If you had any other spouse it would be strange and you would have to become somebody different.

**Very often, victims of abuse, even after escaping one abusive situation go right into another one.**

Very often, victims of abuse, even after escaping one abusive situation go right into another one. This is how strong the spirit of familiarity is. You may even desire to have a spouse you can vent at and yell at from time to time, if that is what you are accustomed to.

If you are aware of how this spirit of familiarity dictates your decision-making, then you can do something about it. You can tell yourself the truth. The truth will set you free from old hurtful habits of thinking. The truth will tell you to stay away from certain familiar personalities and look for more dependable friends. You might feel you are not worthy but that is the very lie not to believe.

When you first leave an abusive spouse you may feel wonderful but the guilt sets in and strangeness. The person you slept with, had your meals with, fought with, is no longer there. He or she had become such a huge part of your life that now is completely empty. If they want you back and beg pitifully for you to return, you need a very strong reason not to go back, or you will, and be stuck all over again. It seems unbelievable how many people go schlepping back, head and shoulders bent low. They just can't picture being apart from the abuser and the abuser smiles and knows they have successfully programmed this person's brain. Even when they could be free they choose not to be.

If you plan to leave someone who mistreats you and controls you constantly, giving you no room to breathe, prepare a list of TRUTHS, that will help you when you are tempted to step back into an abusive relationship. Listen to the loving voice of Jesus. He knows every inch of you and will be a wonderful shepherd to you if you let Him. He will refresh you, and lead you in good and right paths. Even in dark times, He will be beside you and comfort you.

> *"And the Lord guide thee continually, and satisfy thy soul in drought, and make fat thy bones: and thou shalt be like a watered garden, and like a spring of water, whose waters fail not." Isaiah 58:11*

# Check Your Heart

> "Hast thou faith? Have it to thyself before God.
> Happy is the man who condemethnot himself
> in that thing which he alloweth."
> Romans 14:22

Some abusers enforce stringent laws on their victim spouses. They make up new laws continually for their husband or wife to strictly adhere to. Don't push the chair so close to the curtain; don't step on the door ledge; heat up your plate before putting it in the microwave, line up your tins of food by alphabetical order in your cupboard, wear pink on Monday, don't listen to music when you want; speed up, slow down, stop, go , and on and on they demand and command. Some laws might actually make sense but the rule becomes so rigid that there is no room to breathe.

Scriptures tell us that when we are set free in Christ we are free indeed. That might be free to keep certain regulations that we feel are in place or free to refrain from a stiffly regulated life. Eating meat is not sin but for someone who feels it is sin, to him it is sin if he eats it. Read Romans 14.

It's important to check our hearts and why we do what we do if rules are placed upon us it is by choice if we obey them or not. The people who place these rules upon us have their own answering to do in this regard.

If you are living in a difficult situation, taking care of yourself is of utmost importance. There are different ways to get your mind off the rules and on to faith in a God who loves you more than you can comprehend. When you are alone in your car, practice making silly noises, loudly, or sing really loud with the radio, or force yourself to laugh till you are actually roaring with laughter. It will help loosen all the tightness in your body from trying to obey all the man-made laws. After you have done that you might be able to have faith and pray again.

---

---

---

---

---

---

---

---

---

---

## Comfort in Tribulations

"Who comforteth us in all our tribulation,
that we may be able to comfort them which are in any trouble,
by the comfort wherewith we ourselves are comforted of God."
2 Corinthians 1:4

Clare told this story:

Though at her deepest darkest time she could barely speak a word to anyone, God sent people into her life to lift her head. In one church that Clare attended, one lady made a point to greet her every Sunday with a genuine hug and big friendly smile. "She didn't make me talk," said Clare, "but gave me that smile I haven't forgotten to this day. 'God Bless her, wherever she is!'

In another church, there were two young moms who stood out. She called them Cathy and Rhonda. She just had a good feeling when these ladies were at the Ladies Bible Study Class. "I believe now they had the inspiration of the Holy Spirit," she said. She always felt a warm heavenly sensation whenever she was around them. "I accepted this love, which I believe was from God," she smiled, "and I let it flow through me, without a word spoken between us."

In another church, there was a wonderful sister who would come to her after the service and look into her eyes, smiling, would sing her name to her, in a fun way. What a sweet savory aroma this brought to Clare.

There were other churches and places where people blessed her with kind words and loving deeds even though they did not know her situation. "I simply believe," declared Clare, "that they were angels sent from heaven to sprinkle sweet joys into my life. People who genuinely accepted me and loved me even though I might have appeared a bit off kilter to them."

Clare confided, "I really thought I would stay with my difficult spouse till the end of my days. But then one day the tides all turned." The abuser himself took the abuse to another level, and it became apparent to her that she should leave.

Through all her troubles, she has drawn closer to the Lord and has a greater love of His Word than she ever had before. Now she can comfort those in similar situations, and tell them how "The Lord is their Shepherd", and will guide them also through their troubles. There will be light, both in the tunnel for guidance, and at the end of the tunnel, Jesus always beside her.

_____

_____

_____

_____

_____

_____

_____

# *Commitment*

"If I perish I perish."
Esther 4:16

At the possible cost of her life Esther made the commitment to enter into the king's presence and beseech him to spare her people.

How does one come to such a place of commitment? Would we go against what most people would advise? Would we go against our most dearly beloved ones? Would we heed God's call if we aren't even sure where He is taking us? Would we go, if we weren't even sure of what we are doing – blindly saying, "I'll go where you want me to go"? As Abram did, he went out (following God's call) and didn't know where he was going."

We may be in a good place in our life, and we choose to give up the good and right and what is most often viewed as the best ... to what is the Lord's call.

Some people who have stayed in an abusive marriage do make just this kind of commitment and more so. They give up everything they have and everything they are, and all their hopes and dreams and their very own thinking and opinions, and ideas. They lay it all down. They forget dreams altogether. Maybe they wanted to raise their children a certain way but because of the demands of an abusive spouse they do as the abuser dictates. Maybe they dreamed of a peaceful existence in a loving home, but they give it all up for a spotless house where everything is done by the law with no room for enjoyment at all.

Maybe they were excited to have a spouse to have fun with, to touch intimately and enter into a relationship where they truly experienced the ease of one-ship; a 'Garden of Eden' kind of union.

After some years they might even laugh at such lofty expectations. Life with an abuser is more like peddling desperately just to keep breathing.

The keys to a life you were meant to live lie in between the two covers of a very precious book, "The Bible."

Submitting to God, even when you don't know where it will take you is always the place where you want to be. It's no small thing to enter onto the path the Lord has for you. Be prepared to give up your troubles. Be prepared to be nice to the people that irk you the most. Be prepared on the other hand to speak out words that might, on occasion, offend. Be prepared to speak the truth in love. Be prepared to receive blessings you never dreamed possible. Be prepared to do the unexpected on any given day. Be prepared to laugh till tears flow, cry for joy, dance and be awkward, or even sit quietly in God's presence with nothing to say. Mostly be prepared to HEAR from the God of the Universe.

## Demolition

We all have incorrect thinking patterns from time to time. Incorrect thinking patterns are based on lies, and can eventually rob you of peace and joy.

You may have believed a critic when they shamed you, and felt miserable over it. You may have done wrong but even after you fixed the problem you still feel guilty. Maybe your mistake was due to misinformation but embarrassment follows you around.

There are ways to correct wrong thinking.

When you feel this guilt or embarrassment take over, consider the details. We all can get lazy at times or make mistakes, or overlook something, and that is a normal problem. When you are sick, tired or over stressed, your thinking is not as clear as it would be when all is well.

When you can't let go of that accusing spirit, you're basing your guilty feelings on lies.

Accusing spirits can tell you that you are fat when you are a healthy weight. That you're slow when you're really just thoughtful. That you can't do certain things that you would want to do. That you are not good enough. That you can't learn. And so on. Just look at some people with disabilities, who have overcome insurmountable difficulties with practice and determination. We all have things we enjoy learning and other things we never want to learn anyway.

## As a coping mechanism, we all have times we believe a lie.

As a coping mechanism, we all have times we believe a lie. We may do this till we get over the shock of a tragedy. We might live in denial of someone's death until our minds can catch up. Sometimes people develop bad habits of living in a make-believe world, but these are not good habits and should be remedied as soon as the person realizes the dangers. We are not free until we live by the truth.

An abuser might ask, "Can you handle the truth?" meaning that they want to tell you a bunch of evil lies about you and then accuse you for not wanting to hear it. The whole truth is not one sided like this. Truth is always some good and some bad and the whole truth would include both. Telling someone their good things encourages them to do even better so it is much better to focus more on the good. Negative things that we all have and are most sensitive to, can be told sparsely and with as much kindness as possible.

Maybe you've been shamed with words like, "Everyone knows you should ... always put cream in your coffee before you pour it." or, "Why can't you ever learn ... to get in the shower before you turn it on. Such statements are meant to put you down and are not spoken in truth at all.

The best way to fight lies is by telling the living the truth. Don't put on an act or a show. Be humble and don't think too low or too high of yourself. If you have latched on to lies that keep you down there are ways to get rid of these. The Bible calls this Spiritual warfare.

In 2 Corinthians 10:3–5 we are told, "For though we walk in the flesh we do not war after the flesh: (For the weapons of our warfare are not carnal, but mighty through God to the pulling down of strong holds;) Casting down imaginations, and every high thing that exalteth itself against the knowledge of God, and bringing into captivity every thought to the obedience of Christ.

Demolish the lies by casting down imaginations and seeing your life through God's eyes. He loves you. Demolish lies by the Truth.

_____

_____

_____

_____

_____

_____

_____

_____

_____

_____

_____

_____

## Compassionate Jesus

"Howbeit Jesus suffered him not, but saith unto him,
Go home to thy friends, and tell them how great things
the Lord hath done for thee, and
hath had compassion on thee."
Mark 5:19

In the middle of a personal trial you may know the truth very well. You may be quoting scriptures, praying, fighting the devil, and still finding yourself doubting and wavering. Out of that come lies of self-condemnation. "Here we go again", you might be thinking. "Why is God not answering?"

How can anyone quote scripture and waver all at the same time? All the how to's and what for's don't reach to where something clicks into place, where we're back to peace in our soul.

Back off for a minute from all the self-talk, the praying, reciting scriptures and most of all stop fighting with yourself. Go eat that cookie. Decide you're going to stay in bed and not go to work. Stop the fights. Stop everything. It's okay.

Make a decision. File for divorce. Sometimes you just can't fight it any longer, and you go and do what you yourself have called the deadly sin. It is no lie that pride can be a deadlier sin than divorce. "What will people think? What will the church say? But this is my third divorce," you say to yourself. "There must be something terribly wrong with me. I've chosen three husbands that beat me, abuse me, and put me down. They must be right, that I'm stupid. And now you are trying to force the third marriage to hold together? This should not happen to believing Christians," you say to yourself in mockery!

That is right, but this world is broken. It has been broken since the first sin in the Garden of Eden. That does not make divorce okay or over-eating or loving money. Pride is still one of the deadliest sins, and it leads to all manner of other sins, large and small.

Just because I can't get it together doesn't mean that God is wrong or that He doesn't' know what He is doing. Just because we are up against a wall doesn't mean that God is too. We may feel very lost with the God thing and everything. Don't worry, He'll find you. Sometimes it's just time to back off and stand still. While you are standing still, you can repent for your unbelief. It's not that you didn't try hard enough, but that you might have been trying too hard. Faith in God and trying hard in your own strength are opposites.

You've wanted to stop smoking or over-eating. You've prayed. You've quoted scriptures and cast out demons but there you go, just one more cigarette. You did it again, ate too much.

Are you tired of the struggle? Tell it to Jesus. He won't condemn you. Even while you still have that cigarette in your hand, tell it to Jesus. You're filing for divorce; tell it to Jesus. This is not what you wanted but here you are. Pride aside, you admit whatever it is you are hiding and covering up and shoving into your closet a little deeper. Tell it to Jesus.

When you bring your struggles and sins to Him he will reach out His hand of compassion to you. He will help you.

---

---

---

# Confidence

Be good to yourself. Treat yourself as well as you can. See the good that is in you. Build yourself up.

When you live with an abusive person life is so out of whack it is hard to picture how things really should be. Usually, the process of brainwashing happens really quickly and then you are more stuck in your situation than you know. You know more than you think you know but you are brainwashed into thinking you need your abuser to survive and that you couldn't manage without them.

To find your way out of this maze you need to go against the grain. You have to go against what you think should be right. Against what you have come to believe is true.

Trust what you think instinctively. Don't share your thoughts with your abuser. Don't expect this person to ever understand you. Stop believing they are so smart; they just know how to appear that way. Even if they are clever in some ways, they are leaving out truths about themselves.

You are so used to taking care of everyone else, but yourself you leave out. You might be so used to taking care of others that you have no desire to take care of yourself.

**Let yourself feel the pain again. It
means you are still alive.**

If this is the case, you have gone very far off the right path. Slowly make your way back and start today! Focus on any little thing you enjoy doing for yourself. Validate thoughts, desires, and ideas you once had. This is not selfish but you are doing CPR on your mental health condition. You are important and you can't let yourself get so lost that you no longer exist. You'll be like the walking dead if you let that happen.

Also, let yourself feel the pain again. It means you are still alive. Someone has tried to kill you on the inside and that really hurts.

Coming back to life will mean hard work in a different category than you are used to. We all know that nobody works harder than victims of abuse, but begin pointing your work in a different direction. If you can work hard to appease the controller in your life then you have it in you to work hard to revive your own brain.

Is there anything you have neglected to learn because you've been told you can't? Things like managing money, paying the bills, reading a road map, learning the computer, or any number of things you might wish you could do but are too scared to learn? Are you scared you might fail, so you'd rather not try?

If you believe in a God who can make up to you the years you have lost, then you are more than ready to start your life over. With Him, every day is new, and He will help you when you think it is impossible.

> *"Be not afraid of sudden fear, neither of the desolation of the wicked, when it cometh. For the LORD shall be thy confidence, and shall keep thy foot from being taken." Proverbs 3:25–26*

# Can You Imagine?

Can you imagine a life where the person you spend most of your time with is a constant threat to you? It can be the words they say, the look on their faces, the speed of their snap, the way they ignore you, unless they are making demands, second guess all your decisions, if indeed you are allowed to make any.

Their glaring eye is on you all of the time as they watch you like a hawk and correct you unashamedly for any small error. You can't even walk across the room normally without being told what is wrong with you.

When they are not around, you still have the constantly ringing in your ear; words that put you down or give you orders. You don't think for yourself because that could be treachery. You just think, what would they say or want you to do. Your whole brain is taken up by that one thought. That is the only security you have – which is that you must get it right.

Sometimes you step out and try to do something on your own. Just something very small.

You are at the bank and talking to the teller. You have carefully crafted two sentences to say yet you stumble over half the words and forget what you wanted. Every sentence you ever say you have to memorize so that you don't forget what something is called. Like 'hat' or 'cat,' or 'shoe'.

Your palms get sweaty when you have to order a meal at a restaurant or when your spouse lets you choose where to sit – then chases you out of that seat for a better one just one table away.

You are told that for a change they will let you decide what to buy the kids for Christmas but you can't come up with one good idea. Nothing! You feel stupid and wish you had a chance somehow, somewhere, to see who you really are, without that threatening voice in and around you and over you. Somehow you have the feeling you might be okay, but then aren't at all sure.

Once, you tried running away and checking into a motel but your hands were shaking so badly, and you didn't know your license plate number and taking just one hundred dollars out of your account made you feel awful. Your spouse is probably right about how stupid you are. Then you awkwardly drag all the stuff you threw into the car in panic in haste, and you feel clumsy and klutzy and you want to organize your thoughts but you can't decide if you should keep going or even where to go or to go back home with your tail between your legs.

Then you realize you don't know how to put gas into your gas tank and all the time you hear the voices saying how stupid you are. Especially the words, "I told you so!" Even your walk is weird like your feet are tied together at the knee and you worry you'll trip over something.

You always wanted to drive through the prairies where your family lives and here is your golden opportunity. You are almost halfway there but suddenly you think that maybe you'll be like an invalid, and your siblings will have to take care of you and support you possibly and you just don't want to be such a burden. Maybe you are making too big a thing of it all. At least your spouse knows how stupid you are and puts up with it and does everything for you that you are so incapable of doing. So what if they put you down and you have a crazy screaming fight every once in a while. At least no one else knows how stupid you really are. Then you find a pay phone and phone the abuser in your prison home.

The words come through kindly this time and you are given clear instructions how to drive home. And by the way, insurance in the car is running out on this day, so you take it to be the sign that reassures you that it was not meant to be that you leave. Excitedly, you make your way home. The voice on the other side of the line sounded kind and sweet. Giving sweet instructions and now you don't have to worry whether you are doing the right or wrong thing. You have been told and you know now what to do. There is a certain kind of peace that comes over you. You don't have to learn to do the gas or check into a motel or decide where to live or who will take care of you. You have someone at home who will tell you what to do and then you won't have to wonder how you should do your day or week or your life. You will be told and you will know.

But ... you don't know that in a few years the escape will happen for real and it will be a success. You don't know that you will find out that you're really smart. You don't know that you will get some help and then things will come together. You don't know when travelling back home that day that the next time you leave, you will not become an invalid and nobody will need to take care of you. At that time, you did not know that the shakes are normal and the feeling stupid is really very normal and the tripping sensation is just the same, just because you haven't done it before. It is quite normal to feel so ignorant at such a time because you were so many years held captive so that is the real reason that you don't know how to do grown up things at middle age, is because your confidence is so shattered you have none left and haven't had for a very long time. You do not know as you go back to your abuser that all you will need is a bit of help here and there, just at the beginning and then you will be okay. You don't know that one day you will find out who you really are. That you will have no problem shopping for Christmas or buying a house or car and talk to bankers fluently.

You will find out how fast you can learn when you have confidence. You will know that you can make decisions about what is important for you to learn and what doesn't matter if you ever learn. You will know that you can hold your head up high every day and smile and pray and feel God's presence and His help in everything and that you can grow in the Lord, and you can learn more than you ever could imagine. You will know that you can write that book you always wanted to write, that people will buy and read and find help in.

_____

_____

_____

_____

_____

_____

_____

_____

_____

_____

# Electric

> "The voice of the LORD is upon the waters:
> the God of glory thundereth:
> the LORD is upon many waters."
> Psalm 29:3

"The earth was formless and void, and darkness was over the surface of the deep, and the Spirit of God was moving over the surface of the waters." Genesis 1:2

"But it is a spirit in man, And the breath of the Almighty giving them understanding." Job 32:8

"The hand of the LORD was upon me, and carried me out in the spirit of the LORD, and set me down in the midst of the valley which was full of bones, And he said unto me, Son of man, can these bones live? Then said he unto me, Prophesy unto the wind, prophesy, son of man, and say to the wind, Thus saith the LORD GOD: Come from the four winds, O breath, and breathe upon these slain, that they may live. So I prophesied as he commanded me, and the breath came into them, and they lived, and stood up upon their feet, an exceeding great army." Ezekiel 37:1,3,9,10.

"For God hath not given us the spirit of fear; but of power, and of love, and of a sound mind." 2 Timothy 1:7

To connect with the Spirit of the Living Holy God is indeed electrical.

"The Spirit of God hath made me, and the breath of the Almighty hath given me life." Job 33:4

"The thief cometh not, but for to steal, and to kill, and to destroy: I am come that they might have life, and that they might have it more abundantly." John 10:10

The Bible is full of scripture that points to Christ as giver of LIFE AND BREATH. Giver of power and boldness, wisdom and strength. It even states that "When you are weak, then you are strong."

Connecting with the God of the universe is nothing short of electrical, whether you feel it directly or not. So keep your senses open to what He has to say.

If you are in an abusive situation you might want to study verses like these to build your faith. An all-powerful, all-loving Heavenly Father, would love to help you in any difficult situation. Come humbly before Him and He will show you mighty things. He has the answers to your most difficult problems. He may show you how to live with an abuser and survive or He might show you how to get out.

The thief, the devil, only knows how to do three things: steal, kill, and destroy. He does this through His own kind of destructive math. He knows how to subtract the good from your life. He knows Division – how to cause you to be divided and not certain about anything – and Multiplying troubles.

If the Creator God of the Universe can breathe into a field of dead bones and make them alive, He most certainly can touch you and make your life come alive again as well. Just give it all to Him and say, "HERE! Take this mess and I'll watch what wonderful miracle YOU will do with ME!" Amen.

## Whom Can You Trust?

Have you ever been too discouraged to know what to believe in? Is there too much controversy in the churches to settle on where you can comfortably attend? Or maybe you're too comfortable where you are, and you don't want to change even though you don't agree with the preacher or the teachings.

Maybe your life is just too big a mess to see God in it. Maybe it's too much trouble to figure it all out, with too many deceptions in the churches to trust any of them.

"Christians have as many problems as those who don't go to church," you might say. You might see too much legalism and think, "I can't measure up to that kind of life anyway." The churches are dead and there is no life there, just legalism. People comparing and competing, all the love bombing, the hypocrites.

It is a very real problem to see people like pedophiles right in the churches and as long as nobody knows, they can teach Sunday school or even preach. It is downright disgusting, you say, and it is. There are abusers who hit their wives and control the household with an iron fist. Yes, these are in the churches.

At least when you stay outside of the church nobody will have expectations of you that they have of church goers. At least you're not a hypocrite, you might think.

Someone quite unashamedly once said they didn't want to learn too much because then they would be held accountable.

It is surprising how many issues can be solved when you look to Jesus. Declare to him what you can't do or what you can't understand. He will help you. Personally. One on one. Custom made just for you.

You may trust nobody, not even yourself. But God, the Heavenly Father can always be trusted. He is the Rock you can stand on.

One abused woman, Betsy, was so confused by abuse she could not even go to the library to find the right books to help herself. She had tried everything and was backed into a corner that she couldn't get out of. She had no strength. She needed to raise her children but she could barely put one foot in front of the other. She was not granted the liberty to have a nervous breakdown so she became a walking zombie just going through the motions.

She is not alone. What is such a person to do?

Cling to the Word of God. It is your lifeline. When you don't trust anyone, not even your pastor to help you, when you don't have strength to talk to anyone about your insurmountable problems, when you have no strength to go to the library to sort through the massive amounts of information, then go to the Bible and hold on to it. Even one verse can give you strength. God hears your cry and He will send angels and chariots to help you.

"Not by might nor by power but by my Spirit," says the Lord. Zachariah 4:6

When you can't even follow Him properly, He can guide you in the most tender ways. He has ways that are so much better than our own man-made 'goodnesses.' Let Him help you, by His Spirit.

"For the word of God is quick, and powerful, and sharper than any two edged sword, piercing even to the dividing a sunder of soul and spirit, and of the joints and marrow, and is a discerner of the thoughts and intents of the heart." Hebrews 4:12

"There is one lawgiver, who is able to save and to destroy ..." James 4:12

## Depending On God

God doesn't want us to just depend on Him as a last resort...
He wants us to depend on Him for every breath we take.
And ... that kind of dependent life is not stifling. It's liberating!
—Stormie Omartian

"We have come to know and have believed the love which God has
for us. God is love, and the one who abides in love abides in God and
God abides in him." John 4:16

You may have forgotten what love feels like. When in an abusive
situation, a person forgets a lot of things. You may even have forgotten who you are. You have learned to walk the tightrope for your controller due to their harsh demands, and it has nothing to do with love.

It is for reasons to preserve your sanity and for some semblance of
peace, that you try so hard to obey your abuser. You may obsessively
obey all the rules and laws and requests and follow all the winds of
changes, following all the old as well as all the new demands in your
every waking moment. If you are such a victim, you are held captive
mentally and maybe physically. All you can think of is to find more
ways to obey and maybe gain some approval and some peace. It
doesn't work.

Yes, it will upset the apple cart, and make your life a living hell, but
it really would be a good idea to break free from such obsessions. This
person that hangs the weight of two worlds on your shoulders needs
to learn to breathe on their own. If you are the one that lets someone

hold you captive as if you are their last breath of air, you need to pull the plug and let your owner die. Of course this is not literally, but it will feel like it. They will kick and scream for air, so be prepared for that. Realize that you have been trying to pacify these people for your own source of oxygen as well. You might feel like you are going to die as well. It might make a big tornado in your life – but you will live.

Once you are free from such a leech you will feel wonderful, and then you will feel empty. Turn to Jesus, he will fill you with real life. He will show you the next step. He will guide you through the transition and all the endless questions you might have as you start a new life.

Jesus can take care of you, one breath at a time.

# Nobody Can Do it For You (Personal Faith)

"Faith is a positive forward action."
—Daniel Rawding

Martin Luther King Jr. said, "Faith is taking the first step even when you don't see the whole staircase."

And 2 Corinthians 5:7 simply says, "For we walk by faith, not by sight."

The experience of faith is a first-hand experience. There are certain things nobody can do for you. Nobody can chew your food for you, go on vacation for you, or experience a lover's love for you. You may be able to learn second hand, about a great many things, but to experience it yourself is like giving the story blood and bones and muscle, emotions, and feelings.

Some people read the scriptures daily but don't experience what it says. Sometimes it is because there still has been no new birth in them. Another reason might be because the Bible is only being read as a habitual activity and the heart is not in it. There may well be other reasons why scriptures may not speak life to someone.

**When the scriptures do speak it is amazingly simple.**

When the scriptures do speak it is amazingly simple. It could be compared with a glass of cold water when you are thirsty. Enjoying a meal and getting satisfied. It may come as quietly as a summer's breeze or soft as a snowflake in winter. When you read and experience scripture it is so personal and marvelous. Developing an appetite for God's Word will bring streams of unfathomable truths to you. Nobody can do it for you. You can well be watching other Christians and wondering why some can walk around glum most of the time and others even through hard times, have such a bounce in their step, and you just know they have something you want.

Living a Christian life isn't always easy but if you put your faith daily in the Lord and God of the Universe, you just can't stay down for long.

You don't have to be a long time well-seasoned Christian to experience the joys the Lord gives. If you have turned your back on God, you can always turn back again to Him. It's called repenting, and it is a most wonderful word. Rather than saying sorry all day long for all you do wrong, begging God to forgive you, (and by the way, if you have trusted in His shed blood then you are already forgiven and need not beg) try to repent when you have indulged in negativity or gossip or unbelief. It is simple to say 'I repent of ...'" It is not a scary word at all but one that restores your relationship with your Loving Heavenly Father in an instant. He just wants you to be on the same page with Him. There is no need to grovel long over sins because He is faithful and just to forgive us our sins and to cleanse us from all unrighteousness. When you have a restored relationship with your Loving Heavenly Father, then all is well in your world. There is nothing better in all the world than to walk with Jesus! You don't have to die before having a real relationship with Him. You don't have to be old to have a real relationship with Him. You don't have to be sick or in trouble before you call on Him and learn many wonderful things that He can hardly wait to teach you. Even a child can walk and talk with Him and He will tell many wonderful secrets to you and reveal heavenly things to you that even the smartest most educated people don't know. Begin to fall in love with God and His Word today.

# Give Him the Benefit of the Doubt

"Love bears all things, believes all things, hopes all
things, endures all things.
1 Corinthians 13:7

Who gets the benefits of the doubt?

Do you ever feel at your wits' end? Do you ever get stuck for
words? Maybe you've made decisions you shouldn't have and can't
get out without a huge price to pay? Someone else makes a decision, and it affects your whole life and all your dreams and you have
no power over this situation? You're being misunderstood by your
closest friends, and you can't find common ground? You may have
health issues that are devastating, but you can't do a thing about it
and have to accept your disabilities.

Are you in a caustic relationship, and you're in so deep you feel too
crazy to find your way out?

Let's think of snowflakes for a minute. No two are the same. No
two people that ever lived have exactly the same fingerprints. God's
mercies are new every morning. How many new mercies is that in a
year for one person? New means they have never been used before.
They are brand new – and just for you.

Have you ever just used your imagination and thought, maybe
there are many answers to your problems. Have you thought that
you may have some good choices ...if they would just come to mind.

Maybe there could be many good choices on how to deal with your problem.

Don't you think that a loving God who takes such care to make every snowflake different (and snowflakes are just droplets of water, without feelings and personality,) wouldn't He love to help us where we are temporarily stuck?

We know He made the universe and stars beyond accountability, and He named them all ... you get the picture. But what does that have to do with me being stuck for words right now in this moment?

This is where thinking and meditating comes in. When our neatly organized plans and solutions don't cut it, try the God of the universe and see if He has a few solutions we haven't thought of. He might have a few surprises he'd reveal if we gave Him the benefit of your doubt.

## Don't Forget Who You Are

Have you ever been told you are selfish even when you have given till you have no more to give?

Do you find yourself bending over backward till you can bend no farther and wonder if you are doing your best yet? Do you sometimes wonder if you are the crazy one in a relationship and feel helpless and confused? You may even walk the tightrope perfectly but nobody in the relationship is happy.

This is what abuse is. The abusers never wonder if it is them that is making everything unhappy because they are too busy blaming you while themselves always claiming to be right.

**Today, remember who you are – on the inside.**

Move away from those hardships for a moment.

Today, remember who you are – on the inside. Now, regularly step away from this miserable existence and take a bow and a vow. Bow to how much effort you are putting into your relationship to keep it on a somewhat even keel. Maybe you are hanging in there for a job. Maybe you are keeping your children in a somewhat stable situation that they would not have without you. Then take a vow to keep believing in yourself and never give up on yourself and who you are on the inside.

If you like certain music, don't give it up but find small ways to nourish this love. If you play hockey, find a way to play or at least find a way to keep in shape so maybe someday you might take it up again.

You can become creative in your striving to stay sane. Even time in the bathroom could be spent writing short notes for your book. Running on never-ending errands could be part of a way to lose weight and keep in shape. Always having to sit in the back seat and be quiet could be the time to observe the loud know-it-all's. Since they know so much, this could give you an amazing education! They would never know the difference but you would.

The Bible has this encouragement: "Behold, I send you forth as sheep in the midst of wolves: be ye therefore wise as serpents, and harmless as doves." Matthew 10:16.

_____

_____

_____

_____

_____

_____

_____

_____

_____

## He Owns the Cattle

Jonah remembered the Lord
and the Lord rescued him from the whale.
Jonah 2:7–10

Repent and there is hope! Repent before the living God! Vengeance is mine, God says. He is very patient but for some, the time comes ... and no one wants to come under His hand of vengeance.

Jonah remembered the Lord but even after he obeyed the Lord and went and preached to Nineveh to be saved, he still had a bad attitude. He wanted Nineveh to be punished as the Lord promised. The Lord still had to teach him some lessons. In the meantime, Nineveh repented of their sins.

The king of Nineveh and his nobles sent out a decree for repentance. "Let neither man nor beast, herd nor flock, taste anything; do not let them eat, or drink water. But let man and beast be covered with sackcloth, and cry mightily to God; yes, let every one turn from his evil way and from the violence that is in his hands. Who can tell if God will turn and relent, and turn away from His fierce anger, so that we may not perish? Then God saw their works, that they turned from their evil way; and God relented from the disaster that He had said He would bring upon them, and He did not do it." Jonah 3:8–10

God saw their repentant hearts and saved them from disaster. Even the cattle were covered with sackcloth for repentance. God saw they were serious about their change of heart. Both man and beast did not get food or drink, and all cried mightily to God.

This is how powerful repentance is before God. Our change of heart can change the mind of our Father God Almighty! Nineveh's change of heart was so great that they even fasted their animals. God owns cattle and as scripture says, "He owns the cattle on a thousand hills." Psalm 50:10 ... as well as the beasts of the forest.

Even animals know when there is peace around them or not. In the movie *Temple Grandin*, Temple, unlike the cattlemen, could understand the language of the cattle. She could tell when they moo'ed a peaceful moo or when they were terrified.

Cattle will listen to a 'cattle call' and they respond to gentleness and kindness. How much more so, human beings. Jesus calls us gently and he hears our every cry. He is not pleased with violence, and someday those who force or manipulate their control, will give account, if they don't repent.

_____

_____

_____

_____

_____

_____

_____

_____

# Go Ahead, Stir Up The Gifts

"Wherefore I put thee in remembrance
that thou stir up the gift of God,
Which is in thee by the putting on of my hands."
2 Timothy 1:6

What have you done with the one or ten talents God has given you? Go ahead! Use them!

God will multiply what you have if you step out and use what you have. In the Bible story of the man who did not use his one talent, the Lord says, "At least he could have put it in the bank to gain interest." From Matthew 25:27

In another Bible story, God multiplies what was given. A boy brought Him seven loaves and two fish and Jesus fed five thousand people with it.

THERE IS AN ABUNDANCE for everyone who asks! WITH GOD THERE IS ALWAYS AN ABUNDANCE!

Victims of abuse are often so frightened they think they can't do anything worthy. It is not true. It is all a lie. They have talents and gifts God wants them to use, to bless somebody.

Your abusive spouse, as scary and frightening as they seem, are not as fatal as you might think. No matter what you do as a victim, the abuser will always have his or her hysterics. They will be given to fits of rage whenever they feel this is needed, to keep you in line. Don't take the blame for every altercation that happens. They have things planned to keep you afraid. If you are afraid enough, then their calculations will be right on.

## Abusers are so afraid, in fact they think they would die if they lost their victim.

If the victims only knew how afraid their abuser is of them, they would never be frightened of him or her again.

Abusers are so afraid, in fact they think they would die if they lost their victim. They will never admit it but they don't know how to exist without someone to correct and put down.

Abusers do put on a fabulous light show. They certainly know how to make a lot of noise and cause great fear. If anyone, especially their prized possession, their faithful (fearful) spouse, suddenly finds their gifting and becomes more independent, they fear the worst. You need only sidestep a mere inch from the dictated norm, and you most certainly will see them gasping for their next breath. Hold your head up high. Don't shy away from them and shrink in the least. Keep calm and use your giftings with confidence.

Practicing this you will become less afraid every day. God will bless every effort you make to be free, as you keep your eyes on Him. He will help you to use His gifts for His glory and in time you will be richly rewarded.

_____

_____

_____

_____

_____

# God Hates Violence in a Marriage

"And the Spirit and the bride say, Come.
And let him that heareth say, Come.
And let him that is athirst come.
And whosoever will, let him take the water of lifefreely."
Revelation 22:17

What a wonderful invitation to 'come' drink freely. What a breath of fresh air!

In another place, Jesus invites us to 'come' and He will give rest to your souls. Matthew 11:28–30. He desires us to be rested in our souls. "... He maketh us to lie down in green pastures ... beside the still waters." Psalm 23. How marvelous that we have a God who desires for us to have rest and peace.

God does not push or force. He invites, holds out His hand to us, he tells us, He has a good plan for us. But he does not force it upon us. He would that all be Saved, but we know that not all will be saved.

God would that we have pure and lovely marriages and that husbands love their wives and treat them gently. Not all men do that. Women are to respect and honor their husbands but not all women do that.

In Malachi, God is very distraught and infuriated with a people who pretend religion and then weep because He does not hear them. These people practiced things like violence and covering it up. God was very angry with them. Violence and divorce go hand in hand and

God hates it! Even when someone discourages a child, Jesus suggested a remedy. Tie a rock around his neck and throw him into the sea. He completely bypasses divorce.

God would that we stay married and that we do not practice violence and Abuse, but it does happen. Divorce is not the unpardonable sin, but we are a fallen people and sometimes divorce is the only way out of a caustic and sinful situation.

God will not push you into a decision on how to handle the abuse. What He will do is put out his hand to you and say, "Come with me, I will give you all you need. Trust me."

_____

_____

_____

_____

_____

_____

_____

_____

_____

# Hast Thou Commanded the Morning?

"Hast thou commanded the morning since thy days;
and caused the day spring to know his place;
That it might take hold of the ends of the earth, that the
wicked might be shaken out of it."
Job 38:12,13.

Further reading in the end of Job you will find more such questions. Profound statements that even Job could not answer. God gave Job a turn to speak first and you can read about his desperate story in the first thirty-seven chapters of Job. Job was a righteous man. Yet God allowed all his children to be killed and all his cattle and animals to be taken and then himself covered from head to foot with sores and boils. He was a good man, and we might not blame him for some complaining. After all, he was in pain physically, mentally, and emotionally.

In Chapter 38, God begins His speech. It is like another language altogether. He thinks on a much grander scale than Job or any human being. Job talks of his valid complaints, and after all, God allowed much suffering to come his way. Job's troubles are about here and now and himself. Nobody blames him, not even God. But God speaks from a different standpoint.

God was not just on the observation stands. The stars are large and fabulous out there, Job, aren't they? Can you see that ocean over there, isn't it deep and wide? See this dirt here, Job, good dirt indeed. Surely a good place to grow a garden. No, God did not say anything like that. He went straight from man's observation stand to the source.

God's words are found in Job 38–42. "Where were you when I laid the foundations of the earth?" "When I measured it all out?" "Where were you when the stars all sang together?" "Hast thou given the horse strength ..." "Canst thou lift up thy voice to the clouds, that abundance of waters may cover thee?" "Canst thou send lightnings, that they may go, and say unto thee, Here we are?"

He speaks from such a grand place we can only hang open our mouths and feel like a speck on this earth.

Although God is The Almighty one, He did not tell Job he should not speak, to be quiet, to have no voice. Job needed to get it off his chest, and God listened. In the end it was about seeing it God's way. It is important to see it God's way. Our good 'manmade' ways seem right to a man but God sees what we can't see. Even then, He chooses to communicate with us and make His way understandable to those who want to understand. In the end he blessed Job once again but this time with twice what he had had before. In our little worlds, we might see everything only from our point of view. Most decent people, even good church goers, go about doing what they do. They believe in God, go to church, invite people over for dinner and visit the sick and invalid. They may keep a perfect house and pay all their bills regularly. Job was a good man but bad things happened to him. Then God wanted him to see more – much more.

With God, there is always more. You may be in trouble over your head and have no direction on where to go next. You have not found answers in your church. Many of our churches are busy following wonderful agendas and keeping up with the latest popular preachers but are not willing to sink their teeth into real issues and real people. In spite of this dilemma, God has not abandoned those who seek him with all their heart. He came through for Job, and He will come through for you.

Give it all to Him, and He will make your heart dance again.

> *"Thou hast turned for me my mourning into dancing: thou hast put off my sackcloth, and girded me with gladness ... " Psalm 30:11*

_____

_____

_____

_____

_____

_____

_____

_____

_____

_____

## Who is the Accuser?

"And the great dragon was cast out, that old
serpent, called the Devil, and Satan,
which deceiveth the whole world: he was cast out into the earth,
and his angels were cast out with him.
And I heard a loud voice saying in heaven,
Now is come salvation, and strength, and the kingdom of our God,
and the power of his Christ: for the accuser
of our brethren is cast down,
which accused them before our God day and
night. And they overcame him by
the blood of the Lamb, and by the word of
their testimony; and they loved not
their lives unto the death."
Revelation 12:9–11

Christ made a way for all our sins to be erased and completely gone and it was by His shedding of blood that those sins were paid for and all we need to is to believe in Him.

There is truth in the saying, "The devil made me do it." He is the prince of this world, and he goes to and fro across the world seeking whom he may devour. He has no mercy and picks on the smallest and weakest. All he knows how to do is to steal ... destroy ... and to kill. No technique is below him. He even uses Christians who misuse scripture, for his purposes.

A day will come when 'This Accuser' will go to his everlasting destination, to the bottomless pit of hell.

"Be not deceived ..."Galatians 6:7a. To be deceived you must first believe a lie.

"And ye shall know the truth, and the truth shall make you free." John 8:32

Truth is the antidote for deception.

Study the Truth. Know the Truth. Love the Truth. And you shall be free. If you see to the studying and loving ... God will see to it that you will be set FREE!

_____

_____

_____

_____

_____

_____

_____

_____

_____

_____

# God is Not a Bargain Bin

Bargaining with God is natural even for those who don't believe in Him. From times as a child when you really wanted something, up to the time one lays on their deathbed, people often use God as a bargaining bin. What can I get for free? What can I get for dirt cheap? What can I get for begging? What can I get for a bunch of promises? If you let me live, I'll do this and this and this. It is very natural to try to make bargains with God when we are in a tight spot.

To some who don't believe, this will not make sense; but if you give your all to God, no questions asked, free and clear, no promises, just giving yourself and everything you have to Him, He will transform your life like you could never imagine. You must trust Him and give Him free rein before He will do anything for you. What He will do has to be okay, before He can begin His work in you. You don't have to be sick, in trouble, or old first. You don't have to be on your deathbed. God takes you just as you are at any age, in any career you're in, whether you're a perfect angel or behaved all your life like the devil, He will take you exactly as you are, and He will pour His love on you and remake you better than you could imagine.

He does not make bargains because nothing we have could ever be enough for Him, to satisfy Him and His wrath against our sin. He does all the giving, and we do all the receiving. Would you believe that this is possibly the hardest thing for a human being to understand?

Even if all we are is a mess, we want to keep our mess. It is mine, we say, even if it is all garbage. We give excuse after excuse.

You mean we have to shut our brains down? You mean we can't rush around morning to night anymore, working our buns off? You mean we can't compare ourselves with others in order to make ourselves feel good? You mean our good deeds we do, of dedication and love, must end? You mean our love for our children is no good, and we can't please God in any way at all?

Yes, we give up everything but really you don't need to stop doing all that you're doing. You don't need to stop going to school or stop loving your children or stop playing your favorite music. All you have to do is give it all to God. Give your children to God. That doesn't mean that He will snatch them out of your hands, but in reality they are now in better hands than they ever could be. Giving your education to Him will quite automatically become a better and more useful education. Whatever you give to Him, He will do much better with it in your life than you could have done on your own.

So stop bargaining, and give it all to Him. Don't fuss about it, just tell Him you are making a switch, to give Him ownership of all you are and all you have. Next, talk to Him and listen too. It will all become clear, one step at a time. If you have scares and hurts, He will heal you from them. He talks the language of the most simple. Talk to Him and he will make light your heavy heart and give you reason to dance.

Isaiah 61:3 ... to them that mourn ... to give them beauty for ashes, the oil of joy for mourning, the garment of praise for the spirit of heaviness; that they might be called trees of righteousness, the planting of the Lord, that he might be glorified.

# In the Middle of the Mess

God will always work in the middle of the mess.

**Wherever you are, that is where God is.**

Wherever you are, that is where God is. You may be in the middle of dishes, taking out the garbage or visiting a friend. God is there. You may be worried about what you will do after you graduate, or how to find a job or make friends. God is there with you.

Maybe you have some misfortunes; your car broke down unexpectedly or you are out of a job and have a family to support, or your renters trashed the place and now you have to kick them out and spend money fixing the place. Whatever is your situation, God is there with you.

Have you done some stupid things in your life and made some dumb decisions, and now you can't get out of your troubles without a whole life change? Did you start smoking, or stupidly tried drugs or have become an alcoholic; maybe you have ballooned to ninety pounds overweight and losing it is unattainable without a drastic life reconstruction. That's right, God is still smiling at you because He knows He can help you. Nothing is too hard for Him!

There are countless embarrassing situations one can get into and be too ashamed to tell anyone. Countless regrets one can have and you can't change your choices. You may have thought you married the most wonderful loving caring man or woman, but now they end up mistreating you and planning treachery against you. You may have become a doubter in a God that you once loved. Maybe you are aged and feel it is too late. How can you get back to a sure footing? God is there and working in your life even when you might not know it.

> "He is the Rock, his work is perfect: for all his ways are judgment: a God of truth and without iniquity, just and right is He." Deuteronomy 32:4

God is the solid rock we can trust. We can depend on Him and on His word. He even says to count it all joy if we run into trouble. James 1:2–3. Why would that be, so He can laugh at us or put us down for failing Him again? Never! He is a gentleman and kind. When we come to Him, do what you would with a counselor or doctor, discuss it with Him so He can help us.

In Isaiah He says, "Fear thou not; for I am with thee; be not dismayed; for I am thy God: I will strengthen thee; yea, I will help thee; I will uphold thee with the right hand of my righteousness." Isaiah 41:10

Say 'yes' to God in the middle of your mess. That is how to get on the same page with Him. You can express your repentance but sometimes we feel hopeless to turn ourselves around. In fact, it is always best to say 'yes' to God even before you can turn yourself around because then He will help you do the turning. You can say 'yes' even while you still mean 'no'. Keep saying it, He will come to help you.

Keep one eye open to see how He helps. Don't miss it.

# Hitting the Rock

Moses hit the rock and God was displeased. So displeased that Moses was not allowed into the Promised Land.

In Numbers 20:8–12 Moses was angry and when God commanded him to speak to the rock for water to come out, he hit the rock instead and did so in anger. It was not an act of obedience nor of honor to God. Moses was fed up with the children of Israel and had reason to be, but he was to lead God's people in humility and obedience to God. He set a very bad example of how God patiently deals with His people. By looking at their leader, the people would get a wrong impression of how God is and that was very important to our Heavenly Father.

As a leader of a home, the man of the house has a responsibility to be gentle and kind and most of all to be obedient to the gentle voice of the Lord Jesus Christ. Jesus, is a perfect example of leading in patience and love. He had all the powers of heaven and earth yet He was humble and gave His life for sinners. He gives us all the free will to choose whom we will serve. God never forces His will on us but allows us to choose. Freedom is a big deal to God. So much so He allows people to completely ignore the blood He shed on the cross, and His perfect love for us, and choose the wide road that leads to destruction. He lets us choose to what or whom we will bow or give homage to. The priest of the home is to give his life, not suck the life out of his wife and children. There is never an excuse big enough for a man to abuse or put down his wife and children in any way.

To say, "Oh, it's the fault of his wife," is no excuse.

Sometimes, the wife is the abuser but never is he to hit or control her. A true Christian man will continue in gentleness and love even if the situation is extremely difficult. If it becomes impossible he may not have a choice but to leave her but never is it ok to hit or own her.

God created all creatures great and small and to hurt even a fly would not be an honor to the Creator. Some animals are used for food but to hurt and torture is inhumane to the animals. Most people know this but some seem not to have common sense.

To feel sorry for yourself or to have the insatiable desire to overpower another person is a sickness. Sick people belong in hospitals or other places for healing and recovery. There are recovery places for alcoholics, drug addicts, victims of abuse, or even anger management groups. Abusers don't have an anger problem although they are often angry. They have a power issue. They often use anger to overpower another person. They love their power so much they don't ever want to go where they can be healed.

These people are time bombs that feel the need to go off whenever they want, and they use any reason to do so. The best thing you can do is let God deal with them and stay out of the way. The LORD tests the righteous: but the wicked and him that loves violence his soul hates. Psalm 11:5

God disapproved of Moses striking the rock in anger, how much more does He hate violence in marriages and homes!

_____

_____

_____

## Sparkle Like Jewels in a Crown

> "And the LORD their God shall save them in that day
> as the flock of his people:
> for they shall be as the stones of a crown,
> lifted up as an ensign upon his land."
> Zechariah 9:16 NLT

There are crowns mentioned in the Bible that we can receive from God, as rewards for what we have done; crown of righteousness, crown of victory, crown of life, crown of Glory, crown of rejoicing.

"And they shall be Mine, says the LORD of Hosts, in that day when I make up My jewels." Malachi 3:17

Your life may be difficult and you might be lost in your hardship but God knows where you are and to Him you are not at all lost. He may very well be cutting and polishing on you to make you into one of his sparkling jewels. Hardships bring people closer to God's heart. There are times we feel God's presence and all is well. Then just as we are going through a very rough time, He seems to play hide and go seek.

There are many mysteries in the Bible and when we think He is playing hide and go seek, He wants our faith to grow. Sometimes when God seems to be nowhere near us, we may feel this is punishment for something we did wrong. When we suffer and nothing changes when we pray, we might even become angry with Him. What a struggle it is to learn to have faith!

So hang in there when you are in the middle of this struggle. Just tell Him you don't know how to trust but you want to. If you tell Him that it is just too hard; you are still in conversation with Him, and He will count it as faith.

You might remember when you first learned to ride a bike. At some point the one teaching, the teacher must let go of the bike so the child can actually practice riding on their own. But the teacher stays very near as the child swerves and even screams and sometimes falls and scrapes the knees. God never leaves us nor forsakes us and sooner or later we do see Him again as we come through the other side of a faith lesson learned.

Without faith, we cannot please God.

John 6:28–29 says, That our one work that God requires us to do is to have faith. Not preach or teach or work hard at one thing or another – just having faith in Him. Just trust Him, that is what is required of us. And even then He gives us a measure of faith as a gift.

To have faith in the tough times is one of the hardest lessons to learn. This comes with great rewards. Precious jewels, we are, to our Heavenly Father, when we learn to have faith.

## Calm and Courtesy

Children and adults alike respond unbelievably well to kindness and gentleness. Big problems can shrink to manageable size when kind words are applied. To say, "I was wrong" or "I repent", can make all the difference in the world. SMILE at people – and mean what you say.

Calmness, courtesy and kindness; listening, thanking, forgiving; and the list goes on. What do these all have in common?

"Do unto others as you would have them do unto you," and "Love they neighbor as thyself", are both scriptures you can find in the Bible.

"Let nothing be done through strife or vainglory; but in lowliness of mind let each esteem other better than themselves." Philippians 2:3

You don't have to relinquish your beliefs, change your opinions or be a pushover to get along with people. If you are humble and love from the heart, you'll state your views and accept another's, and if it is a heated topic you'll drop it before anyone gets hurt. Other things are more important than being right about everything. Calmness can put much strife to rest.

If you believe in The Loving Heavenly Father, you have everything you need, to be successful in relationships because you can ask Him for help when you need it.

"If any of you lack wisdom, let him ask of God, that giveth to all men liberally, and upbraideth not; and it shall be given him." James 1:5

If someone abuses your calm and courteous manner and uses your kindness for their evil purposes, then walk away. Who says you have to associate with those who prefer altercations and violent speaking or acting? Such people need to learn a lesson, but since they are not the kind that listens to anyone, you must walk away. That is the only lesson they will understand. Maybe someday they will come to their senses and learn something about honesty and treating people with courtesy and kindness.

> *"Do not associate with a man given to anger; or go with a hot-tempered man, or you will learn his ways and find a snare for yourself."* Proverbs 22:25

# When Your Mind Goes Blank

"Wait on the Lord: be of good courage,
and he shall strengthen thine heart:
wait, I say, on the Lord."
Psalm 27:14

Sometimes our mind simply goes blank. Your head is empty. You may be tired. You may have had too much on your mind. There may be too much activity or noise around you, and you find yourself blocking it all out.

Now you feel nothing. Your senses may not be good or particularly bad. You know you had a purpose but it is gone. You had exciting things on your mind, it has vanished. You know the Lord spoke to you and nothing could be more elating. But now you feel nothing.

Maybe you grope around. Lord where are you? Did I do something wrong? Maybe you then blame yourself. Oh yeah, I ate before bed, just what I was not going to do. Oh, that is why I cannot concentrate or feel anything. And I said something to my most wonderful husband, and it wasn't very nice. I wish I had not said that. Maybe that's why I have lost my joy. Maybe I should try harder to go to sleep early. Maybe I should keep the house cleaner, phone my family more, read the Bible more. What do I do when there are these small niggling things that take away my joy?

Maybe it's because the Lord wants me to be still and be like Mary in the Bible who sat at Jesus feet, just wanting to be with Jesus. Just waiting for whatever it is that the Lord has to say to her. We could always sit together and say nothing. What is wrong with that? When He is ready to talk then at least I will be quietly listening.

When you live with an abuser, it could be even more difficult to listen to God. Be assured that He hears your heart whether you say anything or not. Whether you are quiet or whether you cry out, He hears you. Even when you write on a paper all your troubles, and it turns to scribbling that is not legible, and the paper gets torn and crunched and thrown out, still He doesn't throw out what we say. He even stores all your tears in a bottle. Maybe the un-cried tears too.

Try to sit with Him sometime and just say nothing. Mentally give your heart to Him. You might not be able to say those words but make a gesture. He can hear gestures. He can hear your every subconscious thought that you might not even be aware of. He loves you, and He hears your unspoken words. While you wait, be of good courage. He will strengthen your heart.

_____

_____

_____

_____

_____

_____

_____

## God Sends You Flowers

> God hath not promised skies always blue,
> Flower-strewn pathways all our lives through,
> God hath not promised sun without rain,
> Joy without sorrow, peace without pain.
> —Annie Johnson

But He does promise to be with us through our hard times and He does send flowers to us through nature that he created, and other joys and wonderful promises.

From the fall of Adam to this day, the world has been in trouble. One problem is fixed as another is created. New inventions also create new problems. It is the wise and intelligent who will search things out before accepting every new whim.

About the Bereans, scripture says, "These were more noble than those in Thessalonica, in that they received the word with all readiness of mind, and searched the scriptures daily, whether those things were so." Acts 17:11.

Like a bouquet of flowers, God reveals nuggets of wisdom to those who ask.

Sometimes we want to get along with everyone so badly that we become too agreeable. So much so that we would not know if the meek and mild sheep in our presence is really a wolf. "There were also false prophets among the people, just as there will be false teachers among you." 2 Peter 2:1 Scriptures are very clear about what to do when a false doctrine is in our midst.

If there come any unto you, and bring not this doctrine, receive him not into your house, neither bid him God speed. 2 John 1:10

What if this is your spouse? What if this person forces their religion on you, preaching it to you day and night till you grow weary of it. Twisting truth to suit themselves and using sly manipulations or forceful threats to make you walk to their drum beat. What do you do?

Know that your situation is most difficult, not to feel sorry for yourself but gird up your loins with the armor of God. Ephesians 6:10-18. Be prepared to STAND firm. You may do it quietly or sometimes not so quietly, but do not let your heart be bent toward evil, though the situation is thorny.

> "Keep thy heart with all diligence; for out of it are the issues of life." Proverbs 4:23

Even in the middle of chaos watch how God delivers, helps, guides, and gives clarity.

In and among all the chaos He even continues His artwork. There are still beautiful sunsets and sunrises, beautiful flowers and greenery, birds singing and butterflies flitting around, bees buzzing and doing what He called them to do, without any worries.

Whether there are wars abroad or in our homes, stop to notice the flowers God sends your way. It is an act of faith to notice the good that is around us in difficult times. The Lord is the only one to be trusted in uncertain times and He will not let us down.

"Thank you Lord for the flowers."

## He Will Hold Us

"Declaring the end from the beginning, and
From ancient times things which have not been done,
Saying, 'My purpose will be established,
And I will accomplish all My good pleasure."
Isaiah 46:10

To God it makes no difference, whether it be the beginning, the middle or the end. He knows it all and is never purposeless and accomplishes what pleases Himself.

In the middle of trouble, we can't see the end and what good can possibly come out of such a situation. Some even die in an abusive life and never really understood what happened to them or what kind of life they could have had if the victimization had not occurred.

Each of us is only a small piece of God's puzzle and even such a person has a purpose in God's kingdom.

Jeremiah had a calling in his life that not many of us would choose. He was the bearer of 'warning' to a people who didn't listen. God wanted to spare them troubles but they wouldn't hear him. This was Jeremiah's life's work and many hated him.

Sometimes our trouble comes from a calling and a purpose. Other times, it is a result of choosing a path that leads to trouble, knowingly or unknowingly.

Whatever the case may be, God is not purposeless. We may feel at our wits' end but He isn't. When we are in dire straits He can bail us out so fast it would make our heads spin. He can take a messed up life and turn it all around on a dime. God is not bound by time but to us it might seem like forever that He answers.

In that time that you wait, choose to walk close to Him. He can be your comfort, your peace, your light to show you the next step to take. We don't always understand what is happening to us but He does and is the best one to hold us when we are walking through a dark valley.

---

*"The Lord is my shepherd, I shall not want ..."Psalm 23*

---

# Making Difficult Decisions

Are there precious things you're giving up today in hopes the marriage will become better?

Does it keep getting worse though you fervently believe God will fix it all? No one has faith like the abused person. Faith that if only I do this or that, he or she will then be happy, and the marriage will finally be as it was meant to be. Even if it seems impossible, surely God will come and make it all work.

Victims of abuse give up everything. Some have given up ever sitting where they choose in a restaurant. Some give up the truth, and say only what they believe their abuser would want them to say, even to the point of forgetting what they themselves might want to say. They give up their minds. They give up mental, or emotional growth or even spiritual growth in order to do what is dictated. Some give up personal space. Some give up talking. Some give up hoping for a normal sex life, to live a cold and calculated existence. Some give up precious belongings; suddenly what you treasured disappears, and you may never know what happened to it. Some give up the freedom to choose, the freedom to do what brings great pleasure – like sitting and reading, or listening to your favorite music. Some give up the normal joy of planning anything, be it a garden, a trip, a personal passion. All this just to please a demanding spouse. Hoping!

It is very normal when you're in love with someone to become willing to give up things you treasure for the one you love. You want to get along so you seek to please. In fact it may be a pleasure to adjust your life to match his or hers. There is nothing wrong and everything right about such trust. The thing that is wrong is when the next person abuses this trust. But the one who then breaks their part of this trust again and again is the one who must answer before God. You are right when you are abused and turn the other cheek. That is what scripture so nobly instructs us to do and cannot be wrong. But how many cheeks does one person have? When are you giving up enough? When are you giving up too much?

Throughout scripture there is evidence that the Lord seeks to lead and guide and protect from harm. Isaiah 4:5-6 says, "And the Lord will create upon every dwelling place of Mount Zion, and upon her assemblies a cloud and smoke by day, and the shining of a flaming fire by night: for upon all the glory shall be a defence. And there shall be a tabernacle for a shadow in the daytime from the heat, and for a place of refuge, and for a covert from storm and from rain."

God seeks to protect, lead and guide in safety. Even when we don't know where a path is taking us, left in God's hands we can trust it will come to the best kind of end.

Living with an abusive or controlling person is not for the faint-hearted. There is no shame in saying, "I can't bare it any more. Against all my greatest hopes, I cannot do this any longer." Nobody can make that decision for you because only you know when it is enough.

People who have escaped violent marriages, if their lives have come under God's submission, can develop lives full of purpose and usefulness to God.

No, God will not force an abuser to change against their own will, but He still can do a work in you, and give you a double blessing.

> *"For your shame ye shall have double; and for confusion they shall rejoice in their portion: therefore in their land they shall possess the double: everlasting joy shall be unto them. Isaiah 61:7*

---

---

---

---

---

---

---

---

---

---

# Confusion

"For God is not [the author] of confusion, but of peace ..."
1 Corinthians 14:33

One of the first signs of being abused is your feeling of confusion. You lose sight of what is truth and what is a lie. You don't know what voice to listen to. You listen less and less to the little voice inside you and suddenly do not trust it. You may even think you are the reason for the abuse.

An abuser's main goal is to confuse you so they can be in control. Sometimes their controlling method appears quite nice, and you may be lulled to sleep and then one day you realize, like a robot, you are doing all you are told to do. Some controllers gain control by playing helpless or always sick with one ailment or another, and your service to them has no end. Sometimes they lay on the guilt or use religious control. Some abusers use humor to put you down, making you feel stupid. They may tell half truths to confuse you, play mind games, be vague and then say you should understand. You may have agreed too quickly with what they want, not realizing that their goal is to ensnare you.

Especially at the beginning of a relationship, the abuser can be so nice and agreeable; you would never guess their motives. They may play on your weaknesses and appear so much smarter than you. Then when they show love and adoration the victim feels unworthy. Once you are married, the truth begins to come out. Sometimes slowly and sometimes overnight, they turn into monsters.

To an abuser, to have control is like breathing. That is why they are so relentless. They are lost when they can't control. When they feel out of control they will stop at nothing to rope you back in. They may play on your emotions, make you angry, blame you for ridiculous things and make mountains out of any little molehill they can find, to wear you down and take over.

Then they play the roller coaster game. In the first part of the game they are nice. This gives you hope that all will be well after all. Maybe all your efforts paid off and you may wonder why you were so upset. Then they find some small fault in you. You try to ignore the terror that is starting to build inside. Either very quickly or in a few days' time, the tension builds and an outburst happens. The outburst is not consolable although they probably tell you that you should have done this or that and there would not have been a need for the violent altercation, thus blaming it on you.

**Confusion can be overcome by becoming knowledgeable about abuse, by trusting your own instincts, and keeping your knowledge to yourself.**

First being nice, then causing doubts, back to the evil game and then possibly apologies and back to the honeymoon. All this confusion is well planned and rooted in lies.

Confusion can be overcome by becoming knowledgeable about abuse, by trusting your own instincts, and keeping your knowledge to yourself. (The abuser will find crafty ways to put down any newly-acquired knowledge.) If you have nobody to talk to, find someone on the Internet who can relate to you and bounce ideas off these people. Be wise and discerning as to whom you listen to. Gossip and empty complaining will not be beneficial to you.

The Word of God is TRUTH. If you study it you will learn much more than you ever expected because it speaks not only through your mind but also your spirit.

> *"Therefore I love thy commandments above gold; yea, above fine gold." Psalm 119:127*

---

---

---

---

---

---

---

---

---

# Disbelief

"For it is impossible for those who were once enlightened,
and have tasted the heavenly gift,
and have become partakers of the Holy Spirit,
and have tasted the good word of God
and the powers of the age to come, if they fall away,
to renew them again to repentance,
since they crucify again for themselves the Son of
God, and put Him to an open shame."
Hebrews 6:4–6

There are times that for one reason or another people turn away from God. The God they loved and served willingly. The God they loved to thank and sing praises to. Maybe they don't even know why they turn away.

There are many people in the Bible who turned away from God once they were saved. The end of some of these is not clear, while others repent and the relationship is restored. Jobs friends wanted him to curse God and die, when it became unbearable to watch how he suffered.

Peter, in the New Testament, when under the pressure of seeing his friend Jesus about to suffer, denied him and even swore that he never knew Him.

Luke 15 tells the story of a prodigal son who took all his inheritance and left home, squandering all of it until he had nothing left and had to eat in a pigpen with the pigs. There he came to his senses and decided to go back home where his father was watching for him. Seeing him afar off, he ran to meet him, welcoming him home with a spontaneous party and bestowed on him gifts of great value.

This was an example of how our Savior will run to meet us when we are finished squandering all the blessings He gave us that we wasted and took for granted. Sometimes when we are in that place of disbelief it takes losing everything, to come to our senses and know how much we still need our Heavenly Father.

King Saul fell away from God's grace and Solomon backslid after God blessed Him with so much wisdom he was named the wisest man that ever lived.

When Dana was still married to an abusive husband she, in some of her most desperate times, shook her fist at God and cursed Him. "Why did you ever let me live through such misery with no way out?" She damned God, with screams of pain, the same Lord Jesus who came to die for her. Eventually, she drew closer to God, and in time He opened all doors and she actually became free from the abuse. There are those who have backslid and lost their faith in God who read Hebrews 6 and believe they could never be restored to their Lord and Savior. It is a tragic thing to misunderstand that scripture and believe that you have lost your salvation.

I Peter is such a refreshing book to read and over and over talks about the grace of God. We are elected, sanctified, according to the foreknowledge of God. He came to shed His blood for us. It was a gift, free. It explains how the Christian life works, and God is a God full of grace and mercy. We are kept by the power of God and not our own strength.

God does allow us to be tested, and He wants us to 'grow up' in Christ. To believe, even when we feel like He had left us. Take simple steps of faith even if it is just to raise your eyes to heaven when you see the sunshine in the morning or see the smile on your child's face.

If such a thing could happen that you fall away, God would have to die again to save you, but that is impossible. Verses 9–10 of Hebrews 6 continues, " But beloved, we are persuaded BETTER things for you, and things that accompany salvation, though we thus speak.

"For God is not unrighteous to forget your work and labour of love, which ye have ministered to the saints, and do minister. And we desire that every one of you do show the same diligence to FULL ASSURANCE OF HOPE UNTO THE END ... having the FAITH, (not feelings) come to the inheritance."

_____

_____

_____

_____

_____

_____

_____

_____

_____

_____

_____

_____

# When Nothing is Okay, Then Everything is Okay

It is not always easy to understand how God can let us go through such trials that turn us upside down and inside out. What do you do when you just can't find your feet, when you are caught in the spin cycle of the abusers washing machine? How can anything be okay when you are faced with such dread and fear?

There is nothing joyous about living with an abuser. There are panic attacks. There are feelings of hopelessness. One constantly feels stupid and dumb as if every problem is your fault. There is never a sense of growth and change and learning and things getting better. You work like a madman but nothing is good enough. And the discouragements go on day after day after day. How can anything be okay in such a situation?

The schooling of the victim of abuse is not an easy course at all. For God to let you go through such suffering, He has a special plan for you and rewards in heaven. In the moment no suffering is joyous. Hebrews 12:11 says, "Now no chastening for the present seemeth to be joyous, but grievous: nevertheless afterward it yieldeth the peaceable fruit of righteousness unto them which are exercised thereby."

People who have never experienced hardship have little empathy, little understanding of another person, little patience, and are not helpful. They are more like those who get in the way; who know it all, when they know nothing. Those who can laugh and talk, but wouldn't know the difference whether you were a pole or a tree. As long as you say nothing they keep talking.

Most of us don't pay much attention to God and what He has for us until we run into trouble. Like it is said, "There are no atheists in the trenches." And, "Prayer might be outlawed in the schools but they can't outlaw it in the exam room." Troubles draw us closer to God and only when we search for Him and call on Him, do we actually pay attention to what He might have to say to us. He has many wonderful things to show us if we but listen. That could be a reason for our troubles.

God does not want us to be milk and Pablum Christians but to feast on steak and potatoes, vegetables and everything good. He wants us to know how good He can be to us.

When you are in trouble over your head, run to the Lord God Almighty. Commit your all to Him and listen to what He wants to teach you. Take what is at hand, close to you, to find what he wants from you. Always do what you can, and He will show you more. This is how He will guide you one day at a time. Whether you suffer long or short, if you follow Him like this, you will be refined and come out as precious gold, tried in the fires of life.

> *"Bow down thine ear, and hear the words of the wise, and apply thine heart unto my knowledge. For it is a pleasant thing if thou keep them within thee; they shall withal be fitted in thy lips." Proverbs 22:6*

# *What Doesn't Kill You Makes You Stronger*

It is said about abusive type people, "These are people we love to hate and hate to love." But they are here and many of us are married to one like this.

Medical diagnoses for abusers could be anything from Narcissistic to Obsessive Compulsive Personality Disorder; possibly Sociopaths or, Psychopathic disorder, among other possibilities. This writing does not go into medical reasons why some people behave with such cold heartedness, selfishness and are so controlling and why they put such unbearable pain on the person they profess to love. Many articles can be found online and in books describing the behaviors and remedies or lack thereof, of these conditions. Becoming more knowledgeable certainly will help in many ways. The knowledge you gain will aid you in deciding, what you can or cannot do in your situation.

Some questions one might have: Why do they do what they do? Why can you never get through to them? Why is their condition so hard to explain to them? Why don't they ever get it? They seem so normal; why are they so abnormal? Does God have a purpose for them? Can they be saved? Can they change? Do they ever want to change? Can they be a benefit in our lives? Can they be a benefit to society? Can God use them? If you have lived with an abuser you have likely asked such questions as the ones listed.

We all might come up with different answers to these questions. Those that make it through are stronger for it. As Kelly Clarkson sang, "What doesn't kill you makes you stronger." This may well sum up the good that can come out of an abusive relationship.

We know the evil that comes out of an abusive situation. Children are hurt and scarred for life. Families are broken. Some victims of abuse never recover and many die either at the hand of the abuser or suicide or from illnesses related to the abuse. If you make it through the mental and physical torture and get away, you might have a chance to recover.

Still the question remains: can any good come out of an abusive situation?

Becoming knowledgeable about the abuse would be a benefit. Your experience helps you reach out to others in a similar situation. Giving warnings to those about to step into such relationships may prevent a lifetime of pain. Other benefits lie in how you learned to cope. Did you learn to be creative in your coping? Some find helpful therapy in writing or painting, in learning how to find time for your interests when there is no time. You might become very crafty in learning patience, in forgiveness, in turning this big angry ship around to being nice. You might become good in a grammatical sense, in putting on a poker face as to hide your real feelings, which very likely would be used against you if recognized.

Most definitely you have learned to put others first: your abuser in order to try to keep the peace and your children in order to give them some shelter from abuse. Some victims of abuse develop a very close relationship with the Lord as they learn to walk on their knees. You rely more fully on the Lord and experience God's closeness more than most. It is the very thing that carries them through and often out of the vitriolic marriage.

> *"The righteous also shall hold on his way, and he that hath clean hands shall be stronger and stronger."*
> *Job 17:9*

# His Own Lust

"And for this cause God shall send them strong delusion,
that they should believe a lie:
Those who believed not the truth ...
but had pleasure in unrighteousness."
2 Thessalonians 2:11–12.


"But every man is tempted,
when he is drawn away of his own lust, and enticed."
James 1:14

There are as many things to lust after as there are people in this world, including food, fortune, fame, power, adventure, sex, just to name a few. God would have us be filled and satisfied, without constant cravings. He desires to meet all our needs. He would want us to have friends and people who love us and whom we can fellowship with. He can give us all the power we need ... to do His will on this earth. He is all about relationships of the richest kind, and in His plans for us, it might be to have a lifelong spouse, to love honor and enjoy every day for all of our life. But Satan the great deceiver and thief, comes only to steal, kill and to destroy. He mimics and would have us think we can do it on our own. Give ourselves some credit. We happen to love life and as long as we don't have too many problems that keep our head under the water, we say it is of our own making that we are doing so well. God is so merciful and scripture has many stories where He forgives and wipes away sins from our lives. He's the one who gives us breath; and every single day he loves us, meets our needs and blesses us; hears our prayers and heals and saves mankind. But like little children, some of us like to do it ourselves. We want to do good all by ourselves and give ourselves a little credit. This is where pride starts to creep in. Pride comes before a fall, and it is not like we haven't been warned.

Are you a self-made man or woman? You should shudder! There is no such thing on the face of this earth! God made the earth, mankind, and the universe, and lives in and outside of time. He created time and can see all of time at once because He is outside of it. Perhaps He had to travel faster than light in order to create it. Then He created the earth, the dirt that he made man from. Everything runs pretty much as planned and would crumble if it wasn't as precise as it is. He created the universe too and has had it running well. What makes anyone think they are self-made? Could it be pride or self-centeredness? Pride comes before a fall, and this is one time that you can actually predict the future.

Narcissistic people who end up being controlling abusing individuals have made choices in life and have made some pretty bad ones. Many have been given to strong delusion due to constant selfish preferences. They strongly believe a lie. They believe in themselves. They lust after power and find pleasure in it. Eventually, their consciences erode and God gives them over to their lusts. "So be it," He says. "Have it your way."

Whether you are a violent person who no longer feels the full effect of your evil deeds or one who simply says, I don't need God, you need to repent and feel the full effects of your actions.

Humble yourself today! While there is yet time. God holds out His hand even while you are already on your way to hell. "Come back," He calls. "I love you." He will help you stop abusing those who love you and help you to come clean about your self-contentedness.

"Humble yourselves therefore under the mighty hand of God, that he may exalt you in due time." Peter 5:6

_____

_____

_____

_____

_____

_____

_____

_____

_____

_____

_____

_____

## The Ox

"... My yoke is easy and my burden is light."
Matthew 11:30

When you hitch an old ox with a young ox, under the same wooden yoke, the young one will learn from the old ox how to pull the cart. Not to go to the left or the right unless so directed by the driver and what speed to go; not running out of control nor lazily move along, grazing as you go.

This same type of training can work for dogs as well. Dog training can be made easier when you have a young dog with an old, already trained dog.

God wants us harnessed together with Him, under the same yoke; as He says, "My yoke is easy and my burden is light." Of course He carries the bigger load and this is how we can learn from Him, making the learning easier.

He doesn't just stand there and boss us around in a legalistic fashion. He carries the bigger portion and we trust He will guide us right.

Can you picture a loving mother or grandmother taking a child's hand and showing them how to draw a tree or house for the first time. That is how God wants to teach us. When the image vaguely resembles what they are drawing, there are great cheers of accomplishment, and the child is enjoying the journey of learning.

Can you picture this same child being yelled at when the parent just stands over them giving orders. Then when they cannot draw the tree perfectly the first time, they get harshly disciplined. This causes them to become fearful of further learning. They might even catch on eventually, but it leaves a fear element in them that tells them they can't learn.

The Pharisees in the Bible expected more from the people than they could live by. They had the law and lived very religiously by it but it was flawed and uneven. Some things were important to do and others were overlooked. Even their righteousness was as filthy as rags. Even while they legalistically followed the law, they spent more time pointing fingers than understanding the people.

Jesus came alongside people. He healed on the Sabbath, which to the Pharisees was breaking the law. The Law was more important to them than the healing. He sat and talked with the woman at the well who had had five husbands but the one she was with was not her husband. Jesus saved the woman caught in adultery that the Pharisees wanted to stone and put to death. He beckoned the children to come to Him
that the disciples tried to shoo away. He healed the women with the blood issue after she had spent all her money and still wasn't healed.

The Jews of that time had him murdered, breaking many of their own laws to get the job done; but they had to take the body down from the cross before sundown. That was the law that could not be broken.

It's not that the laws and regulations of an abuser are always wrong but as the Pharisees, they forget the part to have mercy and grace. They forget how to talk to their loving spouse and children and how to respect the other person's ways and opinions. They don't seem to know that a marriage is not about law keeping and deciding who is boss but about honoring and respecting and above all loving one another.

Jesus never forces anyone to follow Him. But when we do, there are many blessings He wants to give and many things He wants to teach us.

We may need to be remade but when one person rules over another it usually gets very dirty and mean. Jesus can do the changing in us, but He does it by way of walking with us in love. He doesn't barge in. He doesn't bang on the door. He knocks and waits till we come and let Him in. Then there is an intimate togetherness.

Having a meal or snack or some treat together. Supping together. Not one telling the other what to do but being together and sharing some nourishment together. Revelation 3:20.

Little by little Jesus shows and teaches us how He wants us to be. Patiently, lovingly, He carries the load and helps us with our part. He is all about the journey. Looking to Jesus, keeping our eyes fixed on Him, we cannot lose.

Things might get scary sometimes. Sometimes we don't know where the Lord went because we can't particularly sense His presence. We may feel that things are getting out of hand. Is He playing hide and seek just when we need Him most? It might be like a scary story, a thriller, a mystery, a whodunit episode you are experiencing. You know to trust Him but where is He?

Then He sits down beside the still waters with us and causes us to lay down and take a nap. He knows better than we do when we are too tired to go on. He does all the heavy work and then invites us to take a rest beside the still waters, with Him.

Picture Him with us, and maybe he brought some fish and a loaf of bread, and you tell Him all about it while you spend the time together. There is so much He wants to tell us and teach us. How to get off the Pablum and start enjoying the steak and potatoes.

But all the while He doesn't push. He is like the ox beside us oxen, and pulls most of the load as we carry our lighter part.

## Pollution of Pride

Where is the greatest pollution in the world? Is it pollution in our neighborhoods, in the slums, or in some of the poverty-stricken places in the world?

Pride can be a great polluter. It pollutes the mind and heart of those who are possessed by it. Pride can be obvious or not so obvious in ourselves or others. Pride can say, "I can do it myself, I don't need help"; "I'm a self-made man or woman, I want the credit for myself so I'll do it myself." Pride can be dressed up in the finest money can buy or it can pretend to be more humble than others. It can say, I'm above this job. It can also say I'll do all the dirty work without complaint. Indeed, pride can take on many different faces.

Sometimes, pride shows up in someone who always blames themselves for everything that goes wrong around them, thinking they should have done this or that and living with guilt and regrets. Thinking they should fix it all for everyone. They do not want to be seen in a bad light, and they work day and night to be perfect. It can be going overboard on the nice.

Maybe it's trying to cover for everyone else's mistakes. Not confronting mistakes of others, but rather excusing the poor driving skills of some on the roads, excusing the teenager who hasn't learned to be considerate of others, covering for what the co-worker did wrong so they won't get in trouble. Always being the silent hero and feeling secret pride. Even being piously religious reeks of pride.

Thinking we are better, smarter, thinking we can become godlike, thinking we can progress into super humans. These things can cause us to look down on others.

This is an age where we have technology that would have flabbergasted people in our past. In our little brains this does look amazing, and it is. Remember what Jesus told Pilate – that his power came from God, even the power to have Jesus put to death.

Of ourselves we might look quite advanced in all our works and efforts but in the sight of God it is child's play.

Pride always disappoints. It always brings failures. If there is any satisfaction it always has a cruel ending. It is never enough. It stresses and overworks. There is no peace in pride. The Bible says that pride comes before a fall. As C. S. Lewis said, "Make no mistake about it, pride is the great sin. It is the devil's most effective and destructive tool."

"Pride is your greatest enemy, humility is your greatest friend," said the late John R.W. Stott. Taken from an article "Pride and Humility" by Thomas A. Tarrants Ill, D.Min. Vice President of Ministry, C. S. Lewis Institute.

Jesus invited the poor, the naked and the blind to his feast when nobody had time for Him. He sees the heart and in the heart is where pride resides. It's the one sin that most often keeps us away from truth and God.

> *"We may not always recognize pride in ourselves or others but God looks at the heart." 1 Samuel 16:7. "Give your heart to Him to check and cleanse from pride. Pride serves self and not God. God resists the proud but gives grace to the humble." James 4:6*

# There is No Winning For Losing

There is no winning for losing. The clouds rolled in. Nothing you could do to stop them. You lost the fight before beginning. Then why bother? When things appear differently than they are and there is nothing you can do to change that. You get charged for what you have not done. You get misunderstood. You get misunderstood on purpose to make things look different than they really are. They wear you down. They come at you from every side, fast and furious. You want to say, "This is not me. You must have the wrong person." But they make you quiet. They make you feel like you are to blame for everything.

Sometimes you believe it and sometimes you want to scream, "This is not true!" That is especially painful. They can out talk you, out laugh you, outsmart you, even while your eyes are wide open. They can be so outgoing and friendly they seem like the best friend anyone can ever have. They know everything about everything and when you check it out they are always right. If this is the only day you drive one kilometer more today than you did any other day of this year or last year or the year before, they will know it and question you about it. How did they know when you didn't even know it yourself? How close an eye are they keeping on you anyway?

That is when you really know you have no freedom. You are penned in and hemmed in. Their voice is big. Their body too. Even when their bodies are not, they appear that way. They tower. They talk to the authorities about you, but they say it wrong and put a different spin on it. The authorities are convinced and you are confronted and embarrassed. If you only were perfect. That would solve everything, you think. You want to say they are not perfect either but you can't say it. You want to say that you know what they are

doing but it is like a nightmare. It can't be done. Knitting needles might get broken while you are knitting. You start a sentence and they say, stop stop stop stop, you are wrong. You keep trying and they block you and say sternly, NO! That is not how it is!

They push their weight around with words and with their bodies. They push their weight around with the looks on their faces. They push their weight around with their laughter and friendly gestures, with their funny jokes, with their finger pointing. They push their weight around with their whiplashes in changing topics, changing personalities. With their unutterable cruelness, they do this. They belittle, grasp back at your past failures that they made up and have never forgotten. When you make a real mistake, it's their jackpot. Real sins carry a lot of power for these terrorists. Sometimes they set you up to fail. You can stutter. Turn bitter. Be quiet and listen. You can take notes. You can make lists of every request. You can obey them perfectly and then some. You can be very quiet and mysterious. You can study them and their ways. You can decide to play their game too. You never need to tell them anything. You can learn to have a poker face. You can shut down all your emotions. You can learn to feel nothing, just go through the motions. You can make plans. You can lighten your load, throw out everything you won't need. You can study scriptures and memorize them. You can love the Lord. You can sing loudly when you are alone and pray hard when you are under pressure. The Lord sees everything and knows hearts of man. He sometimes lets things ripen, run their course, but believe me, he sees it all. Payday is coming and you don't want to get in His way.

# Being Awkward

What are some of the emotions we experience? You could include sadness, happiness, depression, delight, fear, courage, excitement – also shyness, confidence and anger. To this list you might want to add 'awkward'. Who doesn't hate awkwardness? Awkwardness is so uncomfortable. It means we are at a loss. In awkwardness things don't fit together. When you say something dumb and you can't seem to straighten it out, your awkwardness shows. It's the times your awkwardness shows that it is most awkward.

Don't think you're a special case just because you do awkward so well. God does not mind awkward because often that is the most truthful place to be. Sin should make us awkward. Pride should cause us to be awkward. Fear makes us awkward.

Good can come out of your clumsiness. When we are fearful we are more likely to run to God. When we are stuck, we are more likely to pray. When we say something embarrassing and foolish, and we can't save face, yes, we pray. (After looking for the nearest place to hide.) We examine ourselves and wonder why this dumb thing keeps happening to you. We may even ask God. That is a perfect place for anyone to be in. Now He can speak, and we may even want to listen. We may even see our need to humble ourselves and repent of our pride.

Some young teenagers might run for cover when they are embarrassed, some make a joke of it, or exaggerate the situation on purpose to cover up insecurity. Some are good at thinking on their feet as they smoothly weasel themselves out of their dilemma. Whether you show it well, or hide it well, it's still an emotional turbulence that shows us our insecurities.

Integrity and uprightness do preserve a person from awkwardness. Wait on the Lord to get you through a misstep or an unintended goof up.

"Let integrity and uprightness preserve me; for I wait on thee." Psalm 25:21 If you temporarily lose your head you can always get it back. Don't self-bash, just be humble about it. Humility goes a long ways, as does repenting sincerely for a mishap. We all fall down, so what else is new? Don't say it didn't happen, and don't say it doesn't matter, but face it with grace. Then move on with a greater measure of humility. As you make your way through an abusive marriage, which often puts you into an awkward place of embarrassment, remember that God's eyes are not closed to your distresses. It is a grievous time for you right now, but God will make your desert places like a garden again. Keep your eyes on the One who will make all your paths straight.

> "For the Lord comforts Zion; he comforts all her waste places and makes her wilderness like Eden, her desert like the garden of the Lord; joy and gladness will be found in her, thanksgiving and the voice of melody." Isaiah 51:3

## Out of the Ashes of Fear

'Fear not' is mentioned 365 times in the Bible, once for every day of the year. "... do not let your hearts be troubled, neither let it be afraid." John 14:27 and, "Fear thou not; for I am with thee: be not dismayed; for I am thy God: I will strengthen thee; yea, I will help thee; yea, I will uphold thee with the right hand of my righteousness." Isaiah 41:10

'Fear not' that someone will break into your house or business; 'fear not' that you will run out of food or money; 'fear not' that there will be a collapse of government or banking systems; 'fear not' to read the whole scriptures; even Revelation or Daniel and the prophesies; 'Fear not' that you won't understand or that you won't be able to learn; 'Fear not' for your children or grandchildren or of sicknesses. 'Fear not' of your abuser.

There are those who would love nothing better than for you to be paralyzed with fear. These may be the very people that were bullies as kids and they never grew out of it. Now they have become the people that abuse their spouses and children. Their childhood crimes have exaggerated to adult barbarism. These are the rapists, child molesters, family abusers of their own children bringing confusion and terror into their families. These are the people that won't repent and change, nor turn from their wicked ways. They can go to church and even preach a sermon but true repentance and turning from evil is not among their abilities.

God is a God who can soften or harden hearts. Watch that you do not continue in what you know is sinful, lest your heart be hardened and you can't repent. Maybe you can't change your own heart but if you cry sincerely to God, He will certainly in His great mercy, help you change.

Fear paralyzes, which is the opposite to clear thinking and problem solving. If you are a victim of abuse, be not afraid. Be not afraid to learn. When your fear goes, your mind will open. You cannot change your abuser, but you can change from being weak and helpless and afraid, to someone who is knowledgeable and strong, trusting the God of the Universe for all your needs.

Rise up from out of the ashes. Don't muck around in despair any more. Don't try to figure out the mind of the abuser any longer. Push all the ugly garbage to the side and ask God to deal with it and begin a new journey. This journey starts with, "I can."

Start small if you have forgotten how to think for yourself. Celebrate every small change you make and every tiny bit you learn. Whether you like to learn about history or love reading novels, or want to learn to write or cook, it is all a step in the right direction. Protect what you know from anyone who would say it is nothing. Just happily keep learning and before long the fears of life will be greatly diminished.

Here is a short story of someone who experienced such a terrible tragedy that her brain went into shock. One devastating tragedy shut her memory down completely. She went to see a doctor about this, and he told her to start writing the tiniest of pieces she could remember about her past. She started small but ended up writing a book about her family's history and in the end she made copies to give each family member. Nobody else in the family kept such records, and it became of great value to everyone.

## Hidden Treasures

What are you struggling with today? With Jesus you will never walk alone.

When you are struggling it might feel like it doesn't matter if there is anyone else with you. You just want the pain to stop and stop now! These might be small annoyances that never cease to plague you or a big mountain-sized pain that does not go away no matter what you do. It may lessen on some days but then escalates again no matter how hopeful you were that it would get better.

When you are in such pain that you don't feel anyone in the world understands, go to Jesus. Go alone and do not share with anyone, especially not your abuser about your special time alone with God.

There is an interesting story in 2 Kings 20 about a King Hezekiah that naively showed all his treasures to the enemies of his kingdom. The prophet Isaiah told him how displeased God was with him and that all would be stolen from him, which then happened.

Be careful to keep your special time just between yourself and God.

## Hide your tiny seed of knowledge and your private time with the Lord, where no one can see it.

If you have nothing to say to God, don't say anything. If you don't know if He is with you, then just sit there alone. He is with you and He may be grieving so hard about your situation He has no words, just like you. Decide where your secret place will be and reserve that for your most troubled issues; and sit quietly alone with Jesus. Keep this a secret between you and God and KNOW He is with you and will reward you openly. Don't make it your concern when the reward will come. Don't even think about it. It might be the only grain of hope you will have but as a seed eventually grows, it will grow. Protect it like an embryo. Protect it like a seed in the ground that has to be in the dark.

If you think it will help to share your secret with your abuser and you will together become a happier couple, it will NOT happen. They will be like the bird that snatches seeds that are not hidden in the ground. They will explain away your helpful knowledge and in some way invade your private time. That is what Satan does, he comes to steal, kill and destroy. Hide your tiny seed of knowledge and your private time with the Lord, where no one can see it. It will be your hidden treasure.

—————————————————————————————

—————————————————————————————

—————————————————————————————

—————————————————————————————

—————————————————————————————

## You Are My Hiding Place

"Thou art my hiding place;
thou shalt preserve me from trouble;
Thou shalt compass me about with
songs of deliverance. Selah."
Psalm 32:7

"But thou, O LORD, art a shield for me;
my glory, and the lifter up of mine head."
Psalm 3:3

Everyone has some precious things in their life that they do not want damaged, destroyed or stolen. These might be pearls and diamonds, valuable collectibles, precious books or paintings. Maybe you own an eye-catching 60s style Ferrari, in candy apple red. You would certainly keep such a vehicle well protected and insured, secured under lock and key, hidden from public view – most of the year.

Our minds are also a very valuable commodity we do not want to lose.

Like the devil who comes to steal, destroy and kill; the controller/domestic abuser, comes into a life to do away with your individuality, your character, and who you are and anything you might be. Their main 'cause' is to take over your mind. They may be doing it knowingly or unknowingly. Their belief is that someone must rule over the other and be in control, and it won't be you. Their every breath hangs on to whether you go down or they go down; and it WILL NOT be them! This is how they think.

### If you are living with or married to an abuser, find ways to protect your mind.

If you are living with or married to an abuser, find ways to protect your mind. Don'twaste your quiet moments fussing over what the abuser wants from you. Do not waste your alone time thinking of how to impress them by baking two dozen pies before noon. There is no way to get along with them anyway. Do just enough to save your skin but no more. Rather take the bits of time you might have to sleep, or watch a brainless show, or eat your favorite dessert. Try to revive some old dreams you once had or make new ones. Protect all you think, plan or dream of and do not share any of it with your abuser spouse. Anything you hold dear, do not share! Become the best protector of precious goods.

It is sad that you need to be secretive toward someone who should be your best friend, but it is much more grievous to have your mind taken away. Never forget that the abuser is unreliable. One day they will be nice and the next they will break promises and hopes. Just while you are in the middle of trying to build some nice times, just when all seems to be going so much better, if it suits them, if it enters their mind, they will bring down the house to make a very quick end to all that is precious to you. So shed a tear for the situation you are in and then make sure you protect what is dearest to you.

Draw close to the Lord of Heaven and "He will hide you under His wings. He will cover you with His feathers. He will make you to lie down and rest deeply, He will sing to you...songs of deliverance. Psalm 91:4, 23:2, 32:7

# Hunter's Guide

For the difficult SEASONS.

Encouragement for Men Who are Abused.

There are many reasons why abused men keep the abuse they are experiencing in their homes very quiet. They might be ashamed for being weak. Maybe as men they think they should be able to shoulder everything. They may feel they should be the strong one, the protector, the one who sets the example in love, the one who can shoulder all the blame or the responsibility of the happiness of their wife and family.

Being worried that you will not be believed is another reason why men don't 'tell'. To keep the treacherous way your wife treats you quiet is a form of protection but it doesn't work in the long run.

It is also to protect children from even worse harm why the victim parent stays with such a person. Often, men lose touch with their children when there is a marriage split. It can be for religious reasons, lacking resources and never time or energy to go looking for these resources, being brainwashed or in denial of the problem that keeps victims from looking for help. Some men cope by keeping busy all the time, but this does not make the problem go away.

The top reason for abuse – whether men or women – is the insatiable craving of the abusive person to have complete control. They will stop at nothing to control you, and yes, murder is not ruled out. For both men and women, there may be good times, to give you hope, but this never works for long. The symptoms of an abuser and the remedies for both men and women are very similar.

There is something called the Jezebel Spirit, which both men or women can possess, is very common among women today. Some of the Jezebel symptoms are as follows:

- Refusing to admit guilt or wrong
- Taking credit for everything
- Using people to do their dirty work
- Withholding information
- Lies convincingly
- Ignores people
- Never gives credit or shows gratitude
- Criticizes everyone
- Loves being the center of attention
- Uses information for leverage
- Spiritualises everything, to be above everyone
- Insubordinate
- Pushy, domineering
- Clairvoyant
- Supernaturally knows and senses information – using it against you
- Commands attention
- Insinuates disapproval …[1]

and the list goes on.

---

[1] Truth in Reality, "Consistent Traits of the Jezebel Spirit. Accessed at: https://truthin-reality.com/2012/09/24/30-consistent-traits-of-the-jezebel-spirit/. Accessed March 5, 2018.

The first rule for a victim of abuse is to take care of yourself. Get back your mental health and confidence through positive self-talk, reading positive material on how to do this, begin to read the scriptures and read them till they grabs you and comforts you. (Don't read it in a legalistic manner because you miss the whole point of scriptures completely if you do that.) The God of the Bible is loving toward the suffering and weak and you need

never be ashamed that you have become a weak and frail man. God will give you back the years your abusive wife has eaten up if you trust Him with it. You will get back your honor, dignity and your strength if you stick close to God and His Word. You will find your way to freedom again.

Talking to someone who understands is also very important. This is even more difficult than taking care of yourself. You may find a link online where only men talk of their abusive situation. Don't give up! That is of most importance in all that you do.

Never retaliate even though the abusive spouse may do everything she can to provoke you. Admittedly, this is also a great difficulty. Look for a way out rather. Pray and go deep into the farthest recesses of your mind to find a path out that is safe for all involved. Be wise as a serpent and harmless as a dove.

Treat your strange and caustic situation as you do learning a new language. We all learned the computer language and so you can learn the language as a victim of abuse. Learning a poker face is one of the first things you might want to learn. You can learn to talk to your spouse without actually saying much. You do not want her to become suspicious. You can share thoughts that sound like they come from your inner heart while never sharing what is really there. Learn to have a life of your own even while running after all of her wishes. Yes, this is also difficult, but remember, this is all part of learning a new language.

Good hunters are quiet, stealthy, and knowledgeable; they have the right equipment and know how to use it at just the right time.

If it helps you, carry a little notebook in your back pocket or any other hiding place where you can make all your 'Hunter's notes.'

> *"Behold, I send you forth as sheep in the midst of wolves: be ye therefore wise as serpents, and harmless as doves."* *Matthew 10:16* *"The Lord God is my strength, and he will make my feet like hinds' feet, and he will make me to walk upon mine high places." Habakkuk 3:19*

# God Only Can Convince the Heart

Both sides of the fence have stories and proofs of a god or no god, and everything in between. Bible scholars can fall away from the faith and people of no faith can come to faith in an almighty God.

Some people are in love with long discussions and can argue very knowledgeably. This can be very impressive to some, and they get washed into great intellectual debates that leave out the heart.

What does this have to do with abuse? Not much except for maybe one thing. It's best not to engage in long conversation with an abuser as it is also not wise to engage in extensive dialogue with someone one who gives little consideration to the person they are talking to.

Generally speaking, very few people can be convinced of anything they wish not to accept. We may try to shove something down someone's throat and temporarily there may be a show of acceptance, but when the conversation is over and the person is gone, you will go back to what you believed in the first place.

This is true for a victim of abuse as well. You may have countless years where you do exactly as the abuser says, but as soon as you have escaped from them, you will very quickly know what you really believe.

This bit of information could save you hours and years of inner turmoil and confusion. Instead of spending endless hours trying to convince someone that will not be convinced, it's about making some decisions. Will you stay with your abusive spouse and obey their every whim even when you disagree with it all? Or will you decide that it is better to leave a caustic relationship?

If you stay, then know that you will never be able to figure out the abuser's actions or motives and trying to convince them to change will never work. It is the harder road but it is your decision and nobody else's.

If you decide to leave the abuser then you will have other problems. If you have children you may have difficulties raising them on your own, but in the long run you will avoid much trouble for them. It is not an easy choice either, but you'll have more freedom to make your own choices and you'll find out you are much more capable than you had thought.

Though people can't convince people, the Holy Spirit can. If you attempt to do the job of the Holy Spirit you will just get in His way. So leave your abuser to the Lord. He only knows what to do with such a person.

> *Psalm 129:2-4 says, "Many a time have they afflicted me from my youth: yet they have not prevailed against me. The plowers plowed upon my back: they made long their furrows. The Lord is righteous: he hath cut asunder the cords of the wicked."*

_____

_____

_____

_____

# I Am Not Alone

"I will instruct thee and teach thee in the way which thou shalt go:
I will guide thee with mine eye."
Psalm 32:8

You are not alone!

Some victims of abuse feel very alone in their corner. They have few close friendships, if any. They don't know that there are people out there who actually understand what they are going through, and that there is help.

Stretch your imagination. There could be a neighbor, a church friend, your family doctor, hairdresser, or even a brother or sister-in-law you could confide in. If they don't help, don't be embarrassed. You have done the bold thing and tried. Test the waters first to see if they are sympathetic. There is nothing to be ashamed of if there are tears. You might even explode if you have kept everything in for too long.

If you had a serious accident in your home you'd do your best to get to the phone and call for help. What the abuser does to you is a serious infliction on the inside. You can't see the blood flowing but the seriousness of the matter is even worse when you can't see it.

Victims of abuse have trusted the wrong person and are paying for it by staying in their captor's snare. The snare might not be noticed as there is food on the table and clothing on their backs and a roof over their heads. They may even go out and go on holidays and smile, but the question is, why are they still all tied up?

It is a type of captivity where they are not allowed to speak to anyone about what goes on behind closed doors. The abuser might be nice at times but they might also blow up at any given time for any invented reason. It's the dirty looks from a spouse that you know can hurt you, the disapproval, the negative body language that threatens. It's the attitude that says, "You must do what I know is right; and even questioning it will put you in danger." So you have learned to tow the line and not even show any pain, nor ever even think of yourself.

It is not too late. Pick up your chains and throw them off. Open your eyes. You are not as stuck as you have let yourself believe. There is a loving Heavenly Father who wants to give you a hand if only you will hold out yours. Lift up those feet when you walk and put a little attitude into your step. That you are bound up by someone else's control may feel very real, but there is a way out. Whether you step out of your entrapment today, or not, you can become free on the inside.

Don't give up when your enemy Satan wants you to stay discouraged and stuck in your rut. Watch how God will open a way when you take the steps that are in front of you. God's directions are never confusing or condemning. He will guide you, even with His eye!

> *"How precious also are thy thoughts unto me, O God! How great is the sum of them! If I should count them, they are more in number than the sand ..."*
> *Psalm 139:17–18a*

# Bondage and Freedom From Bondage

"It is not of yourself ..."
"There is strength in the joy of the Lord."
"Perfect peace for those whose mind is stayed on The Lord."
(Taken from Ephesians 2:8; Psalm 28:7;Isaiah 26:3)

Kerry writes, Bondage was my home. It was where I lived and breathed. It is what I believed to be true. At that time it was very hard to envision a life without it. It was so real I did not know another life but indeed it was around the corner. Looking back from a different point of view. It is now difficult to believe I lived such a life. Truly I don't know how I did it except that the Lord was with me, even though I couldn't feel His presence most of the time.

There was plenty of religion in my home of bondage. Church, the Bible, all kinds of Christian books, Christian friends with whom I talked of the Lord, bowed heads and prayer, church work, striving to be kind and helpful, faithful. Loving, giving, bending over backwards, empathizing with others of a different mindset. These I attempted to practice.

God was there. He was with me in spite of my religious practices. He saw my heart in spite of my feverish efforts to live a life pleasing to God. Efforts to get my ducks all in a row and smile at the same time. I knew there were raindrops of blessings falling around me but a time came when I began to beg for the showers. In desperation seeking the Lord of Heaven and earth for more than just raindrops. More than just a house of religious bondage.

For me he answered all in one day. The journey from there was rapid but not the rapid I had been subjected to but one where God takes you through much in a very short time. It was tough but not the impossible kind. It was a hope-filled tough.

Now, years after the release from religious bondage I am living a joyous life of freedom. Divorce was never my wish or desire, just to be rid of the abuse.

God honored my prayers and I received all the help that I needed when the time came to leave. There were tough days but never the impossible tough that I was so familiar with. All the trials I experienced in learning a new life after divorce were fruitcakes in comparison to the daily stresses of abuse.

There are other stories much like Kerry's where God was there even when we didn't know it. God has purposes for us all even for those whose lives seem to have been wasted. We are only as stuck as we are afraid; and only as stuck as we believe the abuser to be right.

Abusers are not right!

Those who live the life of abuse are stronger than most and God is a whole lot closerto them than we know. God comes to deliver us when we are ready and at just the right time. Studying His Word and falling deeply in love with Him, will speed up the process. Isaiah 43

## Haste Makes Waste

Haste makes waste. How often have you scurried and hurried about and in the process done more damage than good?

On the other hand, when you work in a relaxed manner, unhurried, unworried, you work with confidence and ease. You will see what you couldn't see when in haste. Things come to mind that you would have missed when working so hurriedly. You will do fewer dumb things and in better order. You won't put yourself down but just make a note to do it better next time.

**To be unhurried on the outside you must**
**first become unhurried on the inside.**

Work is much more enjoyable when at ease, even if not everything gets done. More loving decisions get made. When fear is dispelled your creative juices flow more freely. When you take your time you will spot the unusual treasures that are right close to you every day. If this is your daily habit, then in a year or a lifetime, you gather up many good times and good memories.

To be unhurried on the outside you must first become unhurried on the inside.Don't let yourself be hurried into having a miserable day. Haste only brings about guilt, insecurity, frustrations, and disharmony. Some say that one thinks their most clever thoughts when most relaxed, just before you fall asleep.

Abusers very purposefully operate on impatience. They do this for the very reasons that they want you frustrated, insecure, unsure, and dependent on them. They want you feeling like you can't think or make proper decisions so that you will naturally fall into their way of thinking. They even expect you to be able to crawl into their heads and know ahead of time what they want of you. "How many times do I have to tell you...you should know this by now. My what a slow learner you are! I can't depend on you for anything!" and so on. They want your every waking moment, your every thought to be on them. Giving you quiet time, thinking time, is abhorrent to them because you might be able to figure them out. Or figure your way out.

Best for the victim of abuse is to work on being quiet on the inside. "Be still and know that I am God" is a good motto to keep hidden in your heart. "In quietness and confidence is your strength." Another helpful motto is, "The joy of the Lord is my strength." Joy in your heart also upsets the abuser's applecart and makes their knees quiver.

Find times every day to be quiet and gather your thoughts, completely aside from the abuser's expectations. Pull away from their hand rather than play into their hand. Don't feel a bit guilty when not all your work gets done. Just remember, they will be angry with you whether you do as they say or not. They will always find a reason to be displeased so don't pay too much attention.

"Commit thy works unto the Lord and thy thoughts shall be established." Proverbs 16:3 "Also that the soul be without knowledge, it is not good; and he that hasteth with his feet sinneth." Proverbs 19:2

You could say, "Ignorant zeal is worthless", as the MSG translation puts it, and, "haste makes waste".

_____

_____

_____

# Lift Up Your Heads

"And when he heard this, he was very
sorrowful; for he was very rich."
Luke 18:23

God will not beg you to follow Him. He will not tell you over and over what he wants of you. He says it the way it is and then lets us make our choices. "Sell all that thou hast, and distribute unto the poor," is what Jesus said, but the man went away sorrowful.

When in an abusive situation often we learn to re-think too much and when we do listen, we listen to the abuser and not to the real voice that first comes to us.

The abuser's voice can be so loud that no other voice can be heard. When this happens you know something is seriously wrong. Repent and ask God to speak to you again. Ask Him to help you listen. Putting another human being's voice above God's, even if it is your spouse, is wrong. Repent, even if you think you could not help it. Repent, even if you think it was not your fault.

God will not fight you on your choices but those who give Him pre-eminence in their life will reap great benefits. He will take you through all your difficult days one step at a time; as you keep your eyes fixed on Him.

Psalm 121 says it beautifully:

I will lift up mine eyes unto the hills, from whence cometh my help.

My help cometh from the Lord, which made heaven and earth.

He will not suffer thy foot to be moved: he that keepeth thee will not slumber.

Behold, he that keepeth Israel shall neither slumber nor sleep.

The Lord is thy keeper: the Lord is thy shade upon thy right hand.

The sun shall not smite thee by day, nor the moon by night.

The Lord shall preserve thee from all evil: he shall preserve thy soul.

The Lord shall preserve thy going out and thy coming in from this time forth, and even for evermore.

If you are in an abusive relationship you are in the most difficult relationship anyone can be in. People have gone crazy in such relationships. People have bent over backwards till they have no more bend left. People have given up everything in hopes of reviving such a relationship, but the revival is always temporary. If you haven't broken, but have survived, you are one of the strongest people in the world; and ones least noticed or given any credit. Give God the credit for holding you up. Reach out to Him and continue to look up.

Psalm 24:7–10 "Lift up your heads, O ye gates; and be ye lift up, ye everlasting doors; and the King of glory shall come in. Who is this King of glory? The Lord strong and mighty, the Lord mighty in battle.

Lift up your heads, O ye gates; even lift them up, ye everlasting doors; and the King of glory shall come in. Who is this King of glory? The Lord of hosts, he is the King of glory. Selah"

Don't be sorrowful but... lift your heads, for the Lord is strong and mighty in battle and He will fight the battle for you if you give it all over to Him.

# No Secrets

> "And have no fellowship with the
> unfruitful works of darkness,
> but rather reprove them.
> For it is a shame even to speak of those things
> which are done of them in secret."
> Ephesians 5:11–12

Children are being taught not to have secrets. Open communication with your child is a basic, in protecting them against all types of violence, from school bullying, sexual abuse, physical abuse in the home, or attempted kidnapping.

Evil loves darkness and secrecy. The very worst thing a victim of abuse can do is keep the abuse a secret. Evil grows in the dark. Abuse grows and gets worse in secrecy.

Do you feel the need to put on a sweet face in public, which is not your normal visage as you are under the control of an abuser? Does your abusive spouse put on a kind and loving show away from home that is opposite to what they are at home? This is dangerous ground to walk on.

If you are deep into 'acting' out of fear it might take some work to begin telling the truth. Your abuser might be so used to you covering for them and acting like you approve of how they treat you, they will not take lovingly toward your changing to truth telling. It will disturb them greatly and cause inner panic, which leads to tighter control.

They might threaten to hurt you more. Some might threaten suicide or play the sick card, to gain back control. They might even become more devious with their threats like play handling knives or even guns, in your presence.

It takes a great deal of courage to switch to a life of truth, but it is absolutely necessary.

It is time to put away shame and pride. There will be no room to feel insecure. If you have the strength to put up with abuse, you will find the strength to stand up for the truth.

Find friends or a pastor who will understand your position. If they don't, then they are not the ones who can help you. When you find a caring person who can help, ask them to cover you in prayer. Daily prayer. You may need to escape for a time for safety's sake so plan for that. Maybe your friends can help you in this regard.

None of this is for the weak and faint. Don't be ashamed to ask for help. These are not things anyone can bear on their own.

The trickery controllers will stoop to, to keep a tight rein, is downright frightening, which is exactly how they want it. These are sick people, and you have to be careful, and yet this is not the time to freeze in fear.

"Be strong and of good courage, fear not, nor be afraid of them: For the Lord thy God, he it is that doeth go with thee; he will not fail thee, nor forsake thee." Deuteronomy 31:6

"In the day of my trouble I will call upon thee: for thou wilt answer me." Psalm 86:7

If truth cannot be lived in a kind and gentle and loving manner; if truth causes anger and violence; if truth telling causes fear; if your atmosphere is not one of peace with your spouse; consider whether you should be in this place. We all have disagreements and differences and that is normal, but violence and fear are not how a relationship should ever be and are not from God.

Seek Him, he is above the law and when you seek Him humbly and sincerely, He will open up the path to freedom for you. Be ready to step out when the opportunity arises.

## Not Impossible

"Then said he unto the disciples,
It is impossible but that offenses will come:
but woe unto him, through whom they come!"
Luke 17:1

"But whoso shall offend one of these
little ones which believe in me,
it were better for him that a millstone
were hanged about his neck,
and that he were drowned in the depth of the sea."
Matthew 18:6

In the September 7 'Morning by Morning' devotional, written by C. S. Spurgeon in the mid 1800s, he made the ear catching statement, "Faith is full of inventions..." A book titled *Infinitely More* has the heartrending, heart-warming story of Alex Krutov a baby discarded in the garbage in a back ally in Russia, yet lived to tell his story of how God is a God who gives 'infinitely more'.

This is to challenge those who feel they are in a hopeless situation. It is always easier to destroy than to build but build you must! If you have a child that suffers by the hand of an abusive parent it is your duty to keep the child from danger or you are as much to blame for the abuse as is the abuser. If you let yourself be worn down by the abuser, and if you do nothing about it, you must take responsibility for your state of being.

It is true that there are many people in the world who suffer much more severe things than you, but that is no reason for you to lie down and do nothing about your situation. It is not the time for Band-Aids. Abuse is a serious problem and because it plays havoc with your mind it is all the more important to take charge of the situation.

The God and Creator of the universe is so appalled at offences toward children He suggests it would be better such an abusive person be drowned. "Woe unto the person through whom these offences come." The abusers will not get away with their ill treatment of his or her family.

The Creator and Savior of the World requires one to come to Him as a child, if ever they are to make it into heaven. It is true that children need to be trained and taught but it needs to be done in kindness, wisdom, and love. Not with anger offending them and hurting them with confusing language and mixed messages or uncalled-for harsh discipline.

"We then that are strong ought to bear the infirmities of the weak, and not to please ourselves." Romans 15:1 There are rewards in heaven for those who look after those who are weak and yet to those who do not do what they know is right, to him it will be counted as sin. Read, pray, think, talk to people, people in the medical field, search for answers everywhere you go. As Spurgeon said, "Faith is full of inventions." You might invent a safe escape route to save yourself and your children's sanity. God is a creative God and He never runs out of ways to help in a difficult situation. We might think of one or two ways but God has an infinite supply of everything so be looking under every rock and pebble for His answers. While He is answering your prayers He is probably doing a dozen other things like teaching us faith, teaching us creative thinking, developing our gifts and talents.

After He has saved and rescued you, you will also be able to say that God gives 'infinitely more' than we could ever dream or imagine.

# Who Has the Controls?

Raise up higher.

This is not about being above people; not about pride; not about knowing all the answers; but about knowing whom you trust and hold on to, in spite of anything that might happen to you.

Always make sure you are not below your situation or any person. Rise up higher to be on the upper side of things. We all make mistakes. We all get devastated – sometimes due to our own doings. Read through the book of Job, who suffered at the hand of Satan by God's permission. He suffered at the hands of his friends and sadly, at the hands of his wife.

God allowed Job to tell his story; his troubles, his losses, his rejections, his physical pain. He never rejected God, even though it was God who allowed him to go through the pain. The Holy and Almighty God of the Universe called Job righteous! His friends told him to reject God. His wife suggested he curse God and die. In spite of his tragedies he remained believing in his God. He complained, yes! He felt his pain, yes! But he stayed on top of the troubles by continuing to trust the God whom he knew was Holy and completely trustworthy.

After Job had his say and told his story, God had His turn to talk. He didn't invalidate Job but spoke on a different realm all together. He spoke from God's point of view.

God's reply to Job in Job 38–41, comes by some profound questions to get Job to think deeper thoughts. It starts with, "Where were you...?" "Where were you when I laid the foundations of the earth? ... Givest thou the goodly wings unto the peacocks?"... or..." Hast thou given the horse strength? ... Doth the hawk fly by thy wisdom ... Doth the eagle mount up at thy command...?" For four chapters you get to glimpse through the eyes of God.

It is about our positioning. Is God of heaven and earth our foundation we stand on? It is the only solid ground that can be trusted in any situation. It is a wise and righteous thing to trust Him. Any other ground is sinking sand. Our opinions and emotions and knowledge changes every day. Whatever was perfectly good yesterday is new and improved today. Why is it when we are so smart that it always has to be improved on? It couldn't have been so smart in the first place.

Down the path a bit, what we did today, isn't so smart either. Soon we will become gods, some say.

It is not true. It is a delusion and a lie. A 'feeling righteous; daydream of many.' The most sure way of raising yourself higher is to humble yourself and bow in the face of the Almighty. When He lifts you up, you don't have to worry about being less than anyone or below anyone. He will give you the strength to bear trials and He will hold you up in any situation. He will give you strength, for every battle, wisdom for every decision, and peace that surpasses understanding! From Philippians 4:6

---

---

---

---

---

## Proper Barriers

Abusers are good at telling you what is wrong. It takes no brains to find fault and criticize. How much brain work does it take to tell someone the tire is flat, the cookies didn't turn out, or the laundry isn't done, and I need that shirt? Even a child can see that and talk about it. To point out how those cookies should have turned out takes only a pebble of a brain. Those that abuse tear down who you are, and try for the rest of their days, to remake you in their own image.

Try to ignore the obvious put-downs. Keep a clear focus, ignore distractions or things that sidetrack. Put up proper barriers to keep away the devil and his lies.

To find the good in people takes much more effort than it does to find fault. We all have enough faults to satisfy any controller. Try to keep the peace with an abuser and keep your own mind intact. That takes a double portion of strength and nobility.

Sometimes the victor, (victim) uses humor, sometimes they have creative ideas a controller would never have thought. Spending time in prayer, knowing the Creator of the Universe who never runs out of creative ideas, can help you go over the head of the abuser in your life. If you have a direct line to Him you have everything you ever will need.

In the story of Mary and Martha in the Bible, Martha was side-tracked by being busy cooking and cleaning for company. She was right, in that her company was special. Jesus of Nazareth who was

God in the flesh, had come to visit. But Jesus was more pleased with Mary who "sat at His feet and heard His word." Martha fussed over outward appearances and needs. Martha was distracted with THINGS while Mary spent time with her Lord.

Don't let the controller distract you from hearing the still small voice of the Lord. Their words might have "God" in them and "The Bible says", and "You should", and "That just isn't right", but be very discerning. God's voice comes still and soft and very clear.

John 12:28 (NIV) [Jesus prayed,] "Father, glorify your name!" Then a voice came from heaven, "I have glorified it, and will glorify it again." The crowd that was there and heard it said it had thundered; others said an angel had spoken to him ...

There are many voices that can distract us from hearing the real voice of God. God's voice does not compete. Psalm 46:10 says, "Be still, and know that I am God."

1. Proper barriers say NO to abuse.
2. Don't keep secrets. Tell someone trustworthy of what is going on behind closed doors.
3. Do your best to be responsible and don't fall into the trap that says you can't do anything right.
4. We all have faults. Do your best but don't think you need to be perfect.
5. Have a reasonable amount of patience but don't bend over backward till you don't know when to stop.
6. Don't expect to agree with anything one hundred percent.
7. Let your no mean no and your yes, yes. Don't lie to keep a semblance of peace.
8. Ask God for wisdom. It is free for the asking.
9. Learn to recognize that still small voice. The voice of Jesus, is the most loving, caring, helpful voice in time of trouble.
10. Focus on the positives in life and don't waste more time than necessary putting out flames.

# Getting Off the Highway to Hell

Living with an abuser is often like driving at high speeds on a crazy freeway going far too fast.

There is no clear thinking at this pace; to recollect, to focus, to gather one's thoughts, to meditate on the facts. It is very helpful to know the exits or reasons to leave the freeway, ahead of time.

Not having capacity or time to think can lead to poor decisions and craziness and disasters. Very quickly, the garbage in your life adds up and becomes toxic and burns holes into a normal thought pattern. Then you won't know how or when to get off. There are signs on this crazy freeway that point to a way out, to the exits. It is good to know these exit points ahead of time. Each exit is a reason why you should get off. A reason you could use to make a claim for your exiting.

> When life is lived at a breakneck pace and there is no end of this in sight; that is a reason for exiting.

> When criticism is a norm and regular, becoming a cruel way of life, time to exit

> When you no longer are able to think for yourself and you give your brain away, exit.

> When you can never please enough

When truth is gray and you no longer know you are suffering.

When you have turned into a machine; someone else's machine.

When they monopolize your time, money, thoughts, ideas, conversation.

When they use you; your time, money, willingness to help, agreeable nature; with no respect.

When they smile syrupy smiles and give exaggerated appreciations just to use you more.

When they constantly brag about themselves but give you only the dirty look.

When you are required to lie in order to build them up and put yourself down.

When they build you up, just to push you down again.

When you feel strained and drained, empty and dry, have no motivation, no passion, live only for him, or her, no life of your own, sometimes to the point of becoming physically ill; it is way past time to get off the freeway.

Do you feel like nobody cares? Do you feel like you will be alone? Do you feel like you are not smart enough to make it alone? Do you feel like God will turn his back on you and be angry? These are lies.

Hebrews 4:15 says, "For we do not have a high priest who is unable to empathize with our weaknesses..."

_____

_____

_____

_____

_____

_____

_____

_____

_____

_____

_____

_____

## Renewed Like the Eagle

"Praise the LORD, O my soul, and forget not all his benefits –
Who forgives all your sins and heals all your diseases,
who redeems your life from the pit and
crowns you with love and compassion,
who satisfies your desires with good things so that your youth is
renewed like the eagle's.
The LORD works righteousness and justice for all the oppressed."
Psalms 103:2–6

Who would be more oppressed than one who is under someone's cruel and unjust authority and control? This is a cruelty no one can bear. Being under the control of someone who can make right look wrong and wrong right; who says one thing but means another, is heartless. Only someone who disbelieves the victim of abuse, is equal if not more abusive than the actual oppressor.

There is an equal chance for an abuser as for the victim of abuse to be forgiven of all their sins, to be healed, to have their life redeemed. The invitation to be forgiven of your sins is equal to all mankind. Just because there is equal chance does not mean we all take up that chance. If someone rejects this opportunity, not even God can help them.

You may feel sorry for an abuser for their painful childhood but that will not be enough for them to repent of their sins, abusive and otherwise. When you live with an abuser you need to first of all take care of yourself. This may be very difficult but never just lay down and let yourself be owned and destroyed.

Susan grew up with a very meek and mild personality, just what an abuser looks for. Once she was married her new spouse immediately began to physically and emotionally abuse her. She had been so sure that he was the 'one and only' for her, that she decided to stick with him no matter what, believing he would change after seeing her heartfelt efforts. He wore her down so much that eventually she was not even able to carry on a conversation and preferred to stay home and never go out or socialize.

She did eventually get fed up with this kind of life, and she began to go to the library to read books on abuse. She kept her ears and eyes and mind open to learn all she could about such people as her husband. Even though she half believed that she was perhaps mentally delayed, she still continued to search for answers. Little by little she educated herself and little by little she gained confidence in her own abilities.

She knew she could not let her controller know of her searches, so she learned to do all these things quietly while holding up a cheerful front so he would not become suspicious. Eventually, she learned to ask others for help and to trust a few of her friends. They would tell her that she was smart, and their doors were open to help her whenever she needed it. They showed the kind of compassion that the Lord Jesus Christ would show. Eventually, with support groups in place and a Christian counselor, she found a way to leave, and go into the arms of helpful friends.

Today, Susan is helping others in similar situations; encouraging them to trust their instincts, to take care of themselves first and to courageously step away from abuse. The Loving compassion of Jesus is a beautiful thing when seen in Living color of one who lives it.

## *Throw Him Overboard*

Jonah was in the ship when a storm came up and was raging so violently, the men thought they would all surely die. Jonah took the blame and said that they should throw him overboard. Jonah was running from the call of God. After much debate and the sea kept on raging they did as Jonah said. "So they took up Jonah, and cast him forth into the sea: and the sea ceased from her raging." Jonah 1:14–15

Drastic measures are sometimes in place when there is a drastic problem. When you keep on hoping and praying and hoping and praying, it might well be God is trying to tell you something. He may well be telling you that someone needs to be thrown overboard.

This is no small thing but what can one do when someone is continuously threatening us with evil intentions and causing chaos and trouble in a home? It affects the children and is shaping them in a way they should not be shaped. It is stealing life and sucking life out of the other parent. Now two parents are not caring for the young children.

**Wringing one's hands in worry or crying your
eyes out day after day is not trusting God.**

You did not ask for this kind of trouble. You don't even know how to deal with it. This is where trusting God comes in. Wringing one's hands in worry or crying your eyes out day after day is not trusting God. Trusting God is taking steps you don't know how to take. It is not saying that you know what to do but saying, "I don't know what to do but I'll do it anyway. I'll start by taking steps I don't know how to take and keep taking them."

You may not know what to do with a spouse who abuses and never changes. Who is almost nice sometimes but then goes back to old tricks. You may even be sucked into debates you don't want to take part in or worse yet, altercations you never intended. It may well be that the only useful thing you can do in such a situation is to take your children and leave this caustic place. Drastic sins need drastic solutions.

God knew what to do with Jonah when he disobeyed. He knows what to do with your controller. Maybe you don't know, but that is no shame. Listen to the voice inside and have faith. God may need a long time to deal with the person you fell in love with or maybe a short time. That does not depend on you.

All you can do is leave him or her to God. Jonah learned his lesson and repented but only after spending three days and nights in the belly of a whale. A funny story but God is very creative and never runs out of ideas. Take your hands and your mind off your abuser and God will do his work. How and when is not your business. If you leave your spouse that you loved, then expect God to help you with whatever it is you need help with. Make God your partner, and you will learn to deal with loneliness and all other manner of heartaches you never thought you would know you could face.

There are countless scriptures in the Bible that will help you. There are scriptures for every kind of problem so choose the ones that pertain to you. Find promises that bless and help you and hold on to them day and night.

> "Arise; for this matter belongeth unto thee: we also will be with thee: be of good courage, and do it." Ezra 10:4

## It's A Choice

Even those who are in a terrible place make choices. It may seem that the choices are all made for you when you live with someone who breathes the breath of control on you, but think about it again.

The people who suffer most from abuse are the ones who do not take a stand against it. They may cower, bite back, even weep or scream, but their actual voice is not heard. Fear can scream but it can't speak clearly and rationally. Then too, if they ever should be able to think rationally, and attempt to speak, it would all be taken away like a puff of smoke, by the loudness or smoothness of an abuser.

So why try to make choices and be decisive if it is all trodden underfoot, or blown like smoke out a window? Take heart if you are in this position. Taking a stand does not necessarily mean that you make any noise, or that you are always hard.

To take a solid stand is not nearly as hard as fighting the monster. It is a knowing, a trusting, and it is making a decision. No longer will you pretend that all is okay. You may still do most of what the abuser says to do, but in your heart you will have a knowing and that will help you keep your head about you.

If you are decisive, it will not hurt half as much because you will no longer be tossed to and fro like the waves of the sea.

> *"For all people will walk every one in the name of his god, and we will walk in the name of the Lord our God for ever and ever."* Micah 4:5

The choice becomes a little less difficult when you know how much the Lord loves us and has gone all the way for us.

This is nothing about being a strong Christian but about how decisive you are about whom you serve and whom you choose to follow. You may serve your abuser out of necessity but no longer will you give them your heart. We make the decision to make God our master, and He does the rest. So relax. God will bring to you what you need to know.

All you do is make the decision to serve God. He will make a way. Joshua 6:1–27 has the wonderful story of Joshua and his march around the city of Jericho. This is one of many stories in the Bible where God's people believed, and obeyed, and God fought the enemy.

_____

_____

_____

_____

_____

_____

_____

_____

# Running Around in Haste

There is a time to act quickly but in the story of Martha and Mary, Mary chose the better way. She sat at Jesus' feet while Martha was busy and troubled with preparation of dinner for her guests. This story is in Luke 10, end of the chapter.

If Jesus could feed the four thousand in Matthew 15:32–39, He could surely help all of us from scurrying around aimlessly.

Haste makes waste. Hurrying can cause you to make mistakes and then it takes extra time to get the job done.

Have you ever given a gift to someone and they take extra time to look at the gift and appreciate it fully? If it is a book you have given, they spend an hour or two looking at it, reading all the intro's and forward notes. They turn every page and notice all the details on the page. Who wrote the book. The date of its printing. Then when the afternoon is almost over they finally put the book down. They talk about the gift, and you know they have really appreciated what you have given them. They may tell others about this gift and talk to people about the fabulous book they received.

In most cases you get a heartfelt thank you, and you don't really expect more. You are glad they received it and that is good enough for you.

If you are a victim of abuse you might do your best to give thoughtful gifts and go to great lengths to find just the perfect gift for your controlling spouse. Not just that, but you cook and clean and keep the house just as the abuser wants it. When they are unappreciative you wonder what more you could have done. You feel like you have to hold your nose just a certain way when you cook that chicken, or twist your face to the left just so much, while you make that perfect gravy, just so it will turn out as is expected. Maybe the pot handles were pointing just a little too far south and got in the way when a cupboard door was opened or the chair was half an inch closer to the curtain than was expected. Therefore only scowls across the room are forthcoming and that is a thing to be thankful for. At least nobody yelled or got hurt. You might have had two fruits on the table for breakfast but three was the acceptable amount so you failed again. You just can't live without the abuser because you would not know these things without being told.

## When your passion is only to cater to someone who is unappreciative no matter what you do then you are in trouble!

After living like this for several decades, you become somewhat immune to the criticisms and you forget what the true way to live is. You probably hate your life, but living and survival have come to mean the same thing to you. We as humans have a marvellously built-in system to adapt and accept certain ways of life that we are in. We could call it 'the familiar'. Most of the time this serves us very well and helps us live in peace with the ones we love. Once something has become commonplace or familiar, then it seems normal. It feels right, but in some cases it is not.

When your passion is only to cater to someone who is unappreciative no matter what you do then you are in trouble! You live to please them but it always ends up badly sooner or later and you blame yourself for everything, something is going very wrong in your life.

There are people in churches, workplaces, in homes, in stores, on airplanes or anywhere else for that matter, who cannot be happy unless they criticize, find fault and make someone somewhere feel inadequate. If you are running around in haste to please such people, STOP! Yes, STOP! You are chasing the wind, and that is very foolish. Find your place at Jesus' feet, as Mary did, and be at peace. He'll help you get the job done when He, the Almighty, is good and ready. So Relax!

_____

_____

_____

_____

_____

_____

_____

_____

## Ten Were Healed

> "And as he entered into a certain village,
> there met him ten men that were lepers,
> which stood afar off: And they lifted up [their]
> voices, and said, 'Jesus, Master, have
> mercy on us.' And when he saw (them),
> he said unto them, 'Go shew yourselves unto the
> priests.' And it came to pass, that, as they went
> they were cleansed. And one of them,
> when he saw that he was healed, turned back,
> and with a loud voice glorified God, And
> fell down on his face at his feet, giving him thanks:
> and he was a Samaritan."
> Luke 17:12–16

Jesus healed ten lepers in this story. Only one turned back and glorified Him and thanked Him. Still, He healed ten of them.

Even when one's situation is not easy, keep thanking God. Being thankful and positive, opens the mind for possibilities a depressed person would not think of. Don't be ashamed of your situation; don't be embarrassed because God will end up getting the glory for your survival. Psalm 74:21 says, "O let not the oppressed return unashamed: let the poor and needy praise thy name."

If you are in an abusive situation and see no way out, keep a thankful attitude and take steps to do all that you can toward a life of freedom. Don't discuss your plans with your abuser to move toward a positive attitude because they will try even harder to make you miserable. They are insecure and have made their treacherous choices. Just believe in your heart that soon God will show you a way out of your situation. Don't put all your energies into pleasing your abusive spouse. They will never be pleased anyway. God would have you healed and functioning normally so take care of yourself.

Do what you must and that is all. Don't give them your heart and soul. Just do what it takes to keep the devil away from you for as long as possible. You have many times done what Jesus said to do, by turning the other cheek. When there are no more cheeks to turn, other measures must take place. When you know you are wasting your time running after the wind the time comes where your brain will tell you to STOP!

Just ask the Lord to help you forgive them and then carry on with your life.

You might have to take those first steps, as these lepers did, and then by your faith you will be brought out and healed. As you are brought out, don't forget to turn back and thank the Lord for your rescue.

## Some People are So Poor

Some people are so poor that all they have is money.

What could make you happy besides money? Would losing weight or quitting smoking do it? If you stopped worrying about your future or about your safety or about money, you have overcome some of the biggest worries people in this world have. You have been able to 'let go', of what keeps you bound.

"What will people think?" This worry has held more people in confinement in their homes or at work than most other worries. The root of this worry is pride.

One of the most frequently asked question regarding domestic abuse is "Why do people stay?"

Fear might be the biggest reason because the abuser has all manner of ways to inflict fear. They get to know you in order to find out your weaknesses, so they can play their evil power games on you. There could be a fear of what will happen to your family if you leave. All the brainwashing has left you without confidence to even raise your own children.

You may be living a life of make believe as a method of coping. Now you are addicted to this hope, that someday soon your marriage will be blissful and wonderful. It never is and never will be.

This may go hand in hand with the addiction to whining, complaining and telling tall tales to all of your friends. You will get attention and have everyone feel sorry for you. You can't afford to lose the one who feeds your story.

Some victims stay with abusers for religious reasons. The feel very strongly that they will fall out of favor with the God of the Universe should they leave their spouse.

Some victims stay because they have lost a clear picture of what normal life looks like. They are so used to coping that they even pride themselves in coping. Coping is their whole existence.

Sometimes victims are plain lazy. There simply will be too much stuff to learn when they leave. Uprooting is scary. You'll have to change and become responsible. They have a nice house and all the things money can buy, so they stay for their wardrobe or their show off house and besides – they are comfortable in their misery. Some people simply choose to stay poor. Poor, not in money, but in life itself. It's just easier to sit on the couch and cry. Even heaven will be too good for these people.

Irony aside, scripture promises joys unspeakable. "Whom having not seen, ye love, in whom, though now ye see him not, yet believing, ye rejoice with joy unspeakable and full of glory." I Peter 1:8

"... having the glory of God Her brilliance was like a very costly stone, as a stone of crystal-clear jasper. Revelation 21:11

Whether it be getting off the couch or simply fighting against fears your abuser has convinced you to believe, you have a life of unspeakable power and glory waiting if you trust the God of the stars and planets and all heavenly beings as well as Creator of all humankind.

_____

_____

_____

_____

# What Have We Learned?

Our individuality is very precious to each of us, and we all have that inner drive to be our own person. And indeed, we all are unique, and there is no one and never has been one just like us, and never will be.

Even young people who often copy styles and mannerisms of ones that they admire, strangely, do so with the idea that they want to stand out and be different. We detested copying anyone, even our wise elders.

We don't like to be told what to do and we certainly don't want to follow too closely in anyone's footsteps.

We cannot force anyone to make certain choices and most people have made their decisions on things, from what they believe in, to who they vote for, to what they like to eat. We can talk and try to be persuasive but in the end, everyone makes their own decisions on things.

A very common question to a victim of abuse is, "Why do you stay with a person who makes your life miserable every living day?" It does sound silly, and it is. But these are not the only people who make silly decisions.

From one generation to the next, people just don't seem to learn. Kingdoms come and kingdoms die, everywhere from ancient times to modern, and they go through the same steps, from the excitement of pioneering to where they become settled into an affluent society and an intellectual peoples, and then the decline, which includes entitlement thinking, defensive minded, becoming less religious and more self-reliant and so on. Some have studied this pioneering of a nation and its decline, and have noticed that it is strangely very similar throughout the ages right from ancient times to modern.

If we learned a little quicker we would be in a lot less trouble. But we are proud and even if it means staying in a sick relationship we choose to stay.

People go to war and war is always terrible. Young men sign up gladly and bravely. The payment for many is to come home in a coffin. What a tragedy.

There is an eternal choice, heaven or hell. Where do most people choose to go to? The ticket to heaven is paid for in full. A small requirement of faith from us humans but no! Many don't want heaven. They shun the topic at all cost. Those who have experienced the wonderful freedom in Christ would love to see the whole world understand this but really, most people hold their breath when the topic comes up. They have made up their minds. They would rather live in a woolly hairy fairy-tale world than in the Word of God. All religions are the same they say without having experienced the Love of God.

So what is there to do when people choose to stay with an abusive partner and live miserable lives every day?

The answer might come from someone who looked for help and found it. Making the help available might be the best we can do. Pass on what we have learned and just maybe someone will make that choice to escape their disdainful life of abuse and find the freedom they are looking for.

Whether it is a way out of addictions or out of a bad marriage or accepting Jesus into their life, we can lovingly present to others the way. Maybe it will not be accepted today, or they might think about it and come back tomorrow or the next day. Even one soul finding freedom is worth it all.

What Have We Learned?

> "Verily, verily, I say unto you, Whatsover ye shall ask the Father in my name, he will give it you. Hitherto have ye asked nothing in my name: ask and ye shall receive, that your joy may be full." John 16:23–24

_____

_____

_____

_____

_____

_____

_____

_____

_____

_____

_____

_____

_____

_____

_____

## God Will Fight For You

Stand still. Be quiet and move forward. Be still and know ... Therefore stand ...

When God fights for you it can be silent, it can be quick, it can be fearless, it can happen unexpectedly.

Moses answered the people, "Do not be afraid. Stand firm and you will see the deliverance the LORD will bring you today. The Egyptians you see today you will never see again." Exodus 14:13

These verses are not about twiddling one's thumbs. But neither are they about working feverishly but rather like a cat before it pounces on its prey. It is perfectly still. Be still and KNOW that I am God. It speaks of being confident; your step may be slow but it is sure. Watch and pray. Live with expectation. Be alert, not running around crazily.

You may need to run around feverishly when you live with an abuser but there can be two ways of doing this. One is without your head on and full of fear, while the other is with your head on. When you have your head on you know your situation at present is wrong. You follow directions for the moment to keep the peace, but this peace is buying you time to think and pray about your next move.

One thing abusers seldom think of is, that even while you are listening to them or obeying their every wish, that you have a brain, and you can think. They seldom consider that you have a direct line to the God of the Universe who knows your every thought and need. They may think they know what you are thinking, but really, they have no idea at all. They don't know! They act like they know everything but they don't!

They don't know your plans. They don't know that your mind works double time most of the time. Maybe triple time or more. There is the front that you must uphold at all times. It is your 24-hour job and you get no rest from it. Then you have the job of taking care of yourself. This is also extremely difficult while you are living under the total authority of an abuser.

Many victims of abuse completely forget how to do this. Then you have the job of maintaining who you are. Most victims of abuse have only a shred of an idea who they are. They have likes and dislikes, ambitions, hopes and dreams but these only get nourished secretly. There is not much growth in a plant when it is kept in the dark at all times.

Even while these victims of abuse give all their physical and mental time to their abuser they often, while acting out one kind of life, think obsessively of a totally different of life. They are planning how they can do normal everyday things they want without the controller knowing and interfering. They may hide writings. They may have a getaway where they read. They may hide music they love or have secret friendships. They may hide gifts and talents and find creative ways to use them. All of this so they don't lose themselves completely to the abuser. Controllers want control of everything you do and if it ever looks like you are gaining some small bit of freedom they will cut you off from things you love.

Even while victims of abuse may look like they are half-witted or distant or clueless, or if they look like they cannot hear or grasp concepts or if they look like they don't know what is going on around them, they are actually working overtime to live double and triple lives. They may look like they are zoning out during a conversation, but they have better things to do than listen to someone ramble.

May the victims of abuse take heart. You are some of the smartest people on the planet. You juggle better than any juggler in a circus, even while nobody is cheering for you. You are some of the most faithful and the most God-fearing of all people. Keep encouraged to STAND, STAND FIRM, BE EXPECTANT AND READY TO MOVE WHEN THE TIME IS RIGHT, and most of all, KEEP YOUR EYES ON THE LORD GOD who will give the signal.

_____

_____

_____

_____

_____

_____

_____

_____

_____

_____

# The Open Door

> "Behold, I stand at the door, and knock:
> if any man hear my voice, and open the door,
> I will come in to him, and will sup with him,
> and he with me."
> Revelation 3:20

The house was immaculate. Karen worked every day to keep it perfect. Every inch was clean and everything matched perfectly in her home. If the kids dropped even a small toy on the hardwood floor she'd scoop them up and scold them for being careless. Shoes were always straight on the designated shelf by the door. Coats hung straight in the right closet and school bags in their place. This family worked like clockwork ... like robots. They also worked hard to look calm and happy as if they were enjoying their perfect little world.

Lonnie kept a messy house. She was frazzled and joyless. She ran all day to keep up her house as her husband demanded, but it was too much. He'd flare up when he'd see even the tiniest thing out of order, and she tried to please him but it was too much for her. It made her discouraged that she could not please him and the more discouraged she got the worse her house looked. She promised she would do better, but it only got worse. She tried to care, but she felt more like a rag her husband dragged around, than a person.

Steve was young, handsome and athletic. He got married and became Sally's devoted slave. He appeared single minded, pleasing his wife was all that was on this young man's mind. Even when they had guests over, she in her sweet voice would call him to attention and give him little errands to run. You could be sure that he was the one who did most of the housework as well as earn a living. He didn't have a moment's rest, and he did all with a smile on his face.

These three examples could be anyone in the neighborhood. Personalities are Different, and you could not fault them for working hard, being a devoted spouse, keeping an immaculate house.

These three examples also happen to have something in common. They had spouses that controlled them as one would puppets.

Jesus wants to come into our home and have dinner with us. He wants to hear all about our joys and sorrows, dreams, even wants to see what's on our wish list. He likes the 'one on one' friendships and He likes getting really personal. He'd be willing to hear about what's in the deepest hidden away places in your life. Has someone spoken curse words over you and has it affected your life ever since? He'll give you hints on your problem areas. He'll praise you for a job well done that you didn't even think counted. He'll even sing over you, and if you want to get up and dance, He'll probably come and dance with you. Jesus is not the friend that comes only to tell you what a terrible thing you are doing and then leaves. He is not like Satan who lies and makes promises he never keeps. Jesus wants to come in and stay and make Himself comfortable. He brings with Him gifts of peace and joy.

When you will hear His voice, you will love it. He will come to sup with you and you with Him. Sounds like a pretty awesome friendship that is hard to resist.

When you hear Jesus' voice, let him into your home and let Him fix some of your deepest issues. But first of all, He'll probably want to sit down and have tea with you, and become your friend. Work can wait, and besides, when it's time to get to work, He pitches in and helps. It makes the whole job so much easier and so much more enjoyable. Anyone who sees what kind of wonderful friend you have, will want Him as their friend too. You won't have to say much; the joyous look on your face will say it all. Then when the opportunity arises, you might even have a chance to introduce them to Him.

_____

_____

_____

_____

_____

_____

_____

_____

_____

_____

_____

## This Little Light of Mine

"This little light of mine,
I'm gonna let it shine,
let it shine let it shine let it shine.
Hide it under a bush, OH NO!
I'm gonna let it shine ..."

As Scripture states; "Ye are the light of the world. A city that is set on an hill cannot be hid." Matthew 5:14

There are also some strange sounding things written in Scripture about light. "...for Satan himself is transformed into an angel of light." 2 Corinthians 11:14

"But if thine eye be evil, thy whole body shall be full of darkness. If therefore the light that is in thee be darkness, how great is that darkness!" Matthew 6:23

"And the light shineth in darkness; and the darkness comprehended it not." John 1:5

Are you sitting right in the light and you don't know it? This seems like an odd question but it can happen in life. The answer may be right in front of you but you can't see it.

To those sitting every Sunday in churches hearing the true gospel of Christ, have you decided for yourself what you will believe and only hear the scriptures the way you want to hear them? If so, then your ears will be closed to any discernment from the Lord. You might be solidly fixing yourself in the center of your faith, and not God.

## To search for truth is not unbelief.

Have you ever been deceived but think you are believing the God honest truth? If you have, then you will know that that is a greater deception than if you are groping around in the dark. You are indeed fortunate when something jars you awake to the real truth. To have your belief system challenged is a good thing.

To search for truth is not unbelief. To question what you believe or what your church believes is not being faithless. After all, the devil can appear as an angel of light. He may appear to be telling the truth and how he presents it may sound smooth and syrupy wonderful but a lie is still a lie, no matter how good it sounds.

This is not a form of accusation or finger pointing because we all get it wrong sometimes. We may have taken part in the grievous act of adding to the Infallible Word of God or taking from it. That can happen as easily as we sit here. There may have been misunderstandings and misinterpretations of it. Some people have abused what it says, to gain power over another person or maybe a congregation of people. Maybe you have carelessly handled the Word of Truth or maybe you have simply ignored what you've heard it say. It could be that one has fallen into disbelief or even blasphemed against it.

For all of these offences there is hope; for as long as you are alive and breathing you can repent of your errors, and you can be back on the right track with the Lord Jesus, who is merciful, and quick to forgive. To Him, even the darkness is as light and He is the only one who can take your hand of faith and lead you back to the real light.

"Yea, the darkness hideth not from thee; but the night shineth as the day: the darkness and the light are both alike to thee." Psalm 139:12

So quick and willing is God, to restore you to the true Light! "...before they call, I will answer; and while they are yet speaking, I will hear." Isaiah 65:24

# My Voice Shalt Thou Hear in the Morning

"Oh Lord in the morning shall I direct my prayers unto thee and will look up."

Psalm 5 in the Bible, has great comfort for someone in an abusive situation. It starts, "Give ear to my words oh Lord, consider my meditation. Harken unto the voice of my cry, My King and my God....."

Someone who suffers at the control of another, will find deep comfort in this chapter. There is no voice more comforting than when you hear the Loving God and Heavenly Father.

He promises, when you draw near to Him, and put your ear to the ground and listen to what He says, He will let Himself be heard and His voice will be kinder than anything you can imagine.

Psalm 23 "He maketh me to lie down..." He knows when we are so tired we don't know how to relax anymore. This is not how He wants us to work. If we do have much on our plate for a season He will carry us, or give us amazing strength to do what there is for us to do.

Jessica can remember during renovations, how she had to work late into the evening, carrying heavy pails of rock and cement out of their basement that was being renovated. She was too tired to fight. She was too tired to talk or make objections, which would have resulted in altercations she certainly could not handle. It was just all she could do to keep her teeth clenched and keep working. After the rocks were removed, the jobs continued. Now sweep the basement corner to corner. It made no sense since the workers were coming first thing in the morning to mess it all up again. She did all that was expected and then quietly she crawled into bed beside the person who gave her no freedom. He never missed a wink of sleep in all the evil he did.

It was a very long season, her season of abuse. Often, she thought her mind would crack, but again and again she got strength to stand up and keep going.

She had times of happiness in the midst of trouble. When the sun streamed into her window in the morning, when she heard the birds twittering, when the roses began opening their large blooms, when the breeze whisked at her curtains, and she had time for a cup of coffee at her sparkling kitchen table, and read a book. She had times of dancing and singing when she was alone with Jesus and some praise music. There were times when doors of her mind would open a little wider, and she saw more clearly solutions and remedies to her situation – ways to cope and ways to make the lives of her children a little better. There were the good times when friends would visit. There were times when she stepped out of the house to go for a walk in the sunshine or rain. There were holiday times when special people came into her life and made the whole event special.

There were times she heard the voice of the Lord, more clearly and knew what direction to go. Eventually, there were those precious steps that led out of the door for the last time to start a whole new life.

"Oh Lord in the morning shall I direct my prayers unto thee and will look up."

_____

_____

_____

_____

# *Smiling*

Whatever the scientific reason or medical reasons might be, smiling can do miracles.

When the whole world had turned against God, Noah made God smile. When God repented for making mankind, still, "Noah was a pleasure to the Lord." The Lord ended up sparing his life and his family's when the rest of the world went down in the flood.

**A smile is a gift to those it is given to and
lifts the spirits of those around.**

A smile is a gift to those it is given to and lifts the spirits of those around. It can even lift our own spirit if we feel down or discouraged.

A baby's smile can make a room full of adults ooh and aww, laughing excitedly at the pleasure of one simple act of the little baby. A smile can be the first step in a love affair. An approving smile can bring a child confidence. It can boost the spirit of someone who is feeling insecure. A smile can help mend bridges, or heal a hurt. A smile can be a powerful little tool to keep handy. Smiles can attract people to you and they help another to want to be with you. It can help people be comfortable around you. It can be a sign of approval.

Smiles can make people curious about your reason for smiling. Sometimes it might make them suspicious or even jealous.

Zephaniah 3:17, "The Lord your God is with you, He is mighty to save. He will take great delight in you; He will quiet you with His love. He will rejoice over you with singing."

Then on the other hand there are those who think their face might break if they as much as crack a smile. They would sooner drink a cup of vinegar than smile. They make sure those around them don't smile either. They say things like, "You must be lying about something," or, "People who smile a lot can't be trusted." "Only air brains who see the world through rose-colored glasses smile like that." "You must be up to no good," they think, or "You must be hiding something."

"Real life isn't about smiling and being happy," is a statement some abusers have made. "There's work to be done and YOU are the one to be doing it!" "Responsible people don't go around finding frivolous things to be happy about," they say.

This is a definite lie and comes from the pit of hell. In the Bible you will read verses like: "The joy of the Lord is our strength." And God promises, "Joy comes in the morning." After a night of weeping. Psalm 30:5 Even in facing troubles, the Bible tells us to count it all joy when you face troubles ... because it is a test of your faith and "faith worketh patience." James 1:3

When you live with someone who tries to steal your joy, overcome the enemy by finding your joy in the Lord. Joy is a powerful weapon the abuser cannot beat you in. Running after the abuser's demands is like running after the wind. You can never catch it, and soon you are tired and worn out. Rather, find your joy in the Lord, and you will not be wasting your time with emptiness and needless running.

"The Lord reigneth, let the earth rejoice ... His lightening enlightened the world ... the hills melted like wax at the presence of the Lord ...The heavens declared His righteousness and all the people see His glory. Ye that love the Lord hate evil ... Rejoice in the Lord, ye righteous; and give thanks ..." Taken from Psalm 97.

## Take a Step ... By Faith

"And he said to the woman, thy faith hath saved thee; go in peace."
Luke 7:50

Faith takes steps, takes action; faith walks, faith takes the foot off the brake.

There are many steps a victim of abuse can take to make their life better. None of them involve giving your abuser too much attention. That is a good place to start.

**Healthy boundaries balance a relationship."**

Giving any person too much attention will not be good. Healthy boundaries balance a relationship.

If one person does all the talking the person doing all the listening tends to zone out and make no healthy contribution to the conversation. Nobody benefits from such a relationship. Both should seek to take steps to keep from becoming codependent.

Even though no relationship is one hundred percent balanced all the time, both parties work at their end of the bargain. To share the balancing act with all gentleness and kindness is the goal of any healthy friendship.

In an abusive relationship, this is not the case. One of the two parties wants complete control. For the victim of abuse, to gain balance, they continuously must work on taking steps away from the abuser. Abusers do not give space but suffocate, own, and control.

Because it is so difficult to continuously fight this phenomenon, some victims lose themselves in the tight mental and psychological grasp of the controller. To gain even the smallest pebble of peace, complete submission is required. The violence of a controller can cut so deep that victims may remain victims of a phantom controller even long after the actual controller is gone.

For this reason, it is crucial that the victim no longer consider themselves prey, but take daily and regular steps to disengage themselves from the abuser. Don't let your mind slip into flaccid inaction. This does not mean you have to fight all the time with the controller but keep your 'creative thinking' active and protect your most precious commodity, your brain.

Have faith in who you are. Have faith in the Creator of the Universe who made you beautiful, capable, with many creative talents. Have faith in His plans for you, which He will reveal to you, so keep your eyes open. If you take steps every day to keep from being ensnared you will find your purpose and walk in it.

_____

_____

_____

_____

_____

_____

# Difficult Decisions

Some Biblical truths may seem contradictory.

God hates divorce but also God hates violence. Don't have anything to do with a violent man, the Bible says, but what if you are married to one? Does this mean you should stay living with such a person even if murder is on the menu? Maybe not murder; but what if you have to live with the constant threat of angry outbursts and criticisms that would raise anyone's hair on their neck? How serious does the situation have to get before considering leaving? When is someone so brainwashed that they have reached the point of no return? Would a loving God want this for you? Psalm 11:5; Malichi 2:16; Proverbs 22:24–25

You may have a strong faith in God; believing strongly that one should stay married no matter what. You want to do God's will, and you are committed. What can one do when caught between a rock and an extremely hard place?

It is the legalistic Christian that will have the most problem with this. God has not asked us to be legalistic. In fact, to keep the law come hell or high water is not biblical at all. "What shall we do then? Are we to continue in sin that grace may abound?" Romans 6:1.

Living by grace is completely different than living by the law. Living by grace says that you are forgiven undeservedly. That Christ will keep you in the palm of His hand, undeservedly. If you are careless and sin, fellowship with Him is broken but He loves you so much that He will pursue you till you return to Him. All the work is on His shoulders. Our job is to accept His help.

Grace says that we cannot keep ourselves. There is nothing we can do to win His favor. He did it all and all we do is accept it. Yes! Enjoy! With a thankful and grateful heart. God is all about hearts. Nothing about perfection. So back to the divorce issue and living with an abuser.

This sets you free before you even start. A husband or wife should not abuse their spouse. That should help you greatly in making your decision. Whether you stay or leave the abuser, neither is wrong. By Grace, you can do either one of these and walk in freedom.

A good prayer to keep our hearts in check: "Search me, O God, and know my heart: try me, and know my thoughts: And see if there be any wicked way in me, and lead me in the way everlasting." Psalm 139:23–24

_____

_____

_____

_____

_____

_____

_____

## What If We are Broken and Stinky?

God uses broken people. So don't worry if you break down now and then. Don't worry if you fail now and then. Don't worry if you make some wrong moves. Oh, doesn't that sound careless or risky? Yes! But it also spells joy in our imperfection because we won't have to sit so tight and worry about every mistake.

The Bible is full of broken and stinky people. Our own righteousness stinks like filthy rags. (from Isaiah 64:6) For the broken or stinky, there is hope if the broken pieces are brought to God to deal with.

So it may not look like God should have a plan and a purpose for some divorced people, or if you get into trouble with drugs, alcohol, or women. There's nothing for you to do but sit at home on a shelf, smile, and don't move. Have you ever heard it said, "You're divorced, you can't serve here or there in the church?" Yes, but your money is still good, we'll take that from you, divorced or not.

That's not how God of the Bible sees it. There are just too many places in the Bible where God uses the unlikely. He used anything that walks basically. Even Balaam's ass. He used the harlots, tax collectors, thieves, fishermen, women, children, those of little faith, the broken, the sick, the murderer, the self-righteous, the bossy, the wimps, even the rich sometimes.

God is a God of hope. He can still make something beautiful out of something broken and that alone could give hope to anybody nowadays.

Just lay down your life, 'as is', and give it to Jesus. He will make you rich, beyond what money can buy. He will fix what is broken and clean up what smells rotten. He'll even replace the years the locusts have eaten.

> *"And I will restore to you the years that the locust hath eaten, the cankerworm, and the caterpillar, and the palmerworm, my great army which I sent among you. And ye shall eat in plenty, and be satisfied, and praise the name of the LORD your God, that hath dealt wondrously with you: and my people shall never be ashamed." Joel 2:25–26*

## Watch for the Foxes

"Take us the foxes, the little foxes, that spoil the vines:
for our vines have tender grapes."
Song of Solomon 2:15

Do you have things, small things that keep on hindering your joy? Is there stuff in your life that you wish would just disappear? Is it insomnia? Do you constantly fear someone breaking into your home? Do you have to do everything in rituals? Do you think your house is never clean enough? Do you have a constant nagging in your stomach that you should be working harder and get more done in a day? It never leaves you, and you somehow always fall short. Maybe you dislike your figure or looks.

Are there small annoyances with yourself or others that you live with daily? How do you make it stop? Are you fearful of people; of making mistakes; of not being as knowledgeable as the next person; being forgetful; of getting lost in traffic; fear of flying; fear of crowds?

Some people feel they must be in control, or the world will fall apart. Others let themselves be told off, walked on, bossed around and all they can ever do is stutter and look stupid.

Do you think God doesn't care or even hears your prayers when these problems persist? It may not be the impossible large problems that spoil your day, but the tiny, nagging ones.

There aren't any pat answers but we can do some research here. Satan is alive and well on planet Earth. He works extra hard to mess with your life whether you are a Christian or not. He can do only three things: steal, kill, destroy. He has no mercy, and he is a liar.

God has all the answers, all the power, all the love and everything good. How on earth does this 'God' thing work? Does He actually care if we eat right, or try to quit smoking or live in depression?

The key thing about God is that you've got to get on His page before He can do anything for you. When you call the plumber or mechanic for help you expect that they know more than you do about the pipes in your house or about your car. They do their job fixing the problem, and we listen very closely to what they tell us to do in these regards. That is also the basic truth about God Almighty. TRUST that He knows more than you do about your situation. His handbook is the BIBLE. Read it often, and in time you will learn about Him and how He thinks. If you don't understand it, DON'T GIVE UP. Take what you do understand and BUILD on that. TALK to God like you would to a person, not religiously. Ask Him questions. Once you discover His voice and how He talks, you will learn so much that you won't be able to contain it. Getting to know your wonderful Heavenly Father will take a lifetime, but He will be glad to show you amazing things as soon as you start. Look for signposts, treasures, clues, hints, and don't miss the 'easy to see' answers.

Meditating on the scriptures will keep out the many foxes that want to come and destroy your happiness.

"God is our refuge and strength, a very present help in trouble." Psalms 46:1

"I will both lay me down in peace, and sleep: for thou, Lord, only makest me dwell in safety." Psalm 4:8

"I can do all things through Christ who strengthens me." Philippians 4:13

"These things I have spoken unto you, that in me ye might have peace. In the world ye shall have tribulation: but be of good cheer; I have overcome the world." John 16:33

"For God hath not given us the spirit of fear; but of power, and of love, and of a sound mind. 2 Timothy 1:7

Be of good courage, and he shall strengthen your heart, all ye that hope in the Lord. Psalm 31:24

_____

_____

_____

_____

_____

_____

_____

_____

_____

_____

_____

# Water the Flowers, Pull the Weeds

To keep a beautiful garden it is a regular job to water the garden and pull the weeds. There are many other things one can do to make a flower garden bloom and vegetable garden produce beautiful vegetables. You keep out the pesky bugs, nourish the plants with the correct fertilizer, pick out deadheads and thin out vegetables that grow too close together. You read directions before you buy and plant, getting the correct plants for the places you want them to grow. Some plants grow better in sunlight and warmth and other plants do very well in shade or cooler climates.

Relationships between two people work much the same way. To respect and honor each other would be near the top of the list of important ways to grow a good relationship. To put each other first, above children and friends, is also a key ingredient to keeping a happy relationship.

> **To respect and honor each other would be near the top of the list of important ways to grow a good relationship.**

A young couple is told that for good communication, speaking truthfully and kindly is of ultimate importance. This may need to be learned but with practice and a heart that is pure, this does not take long to accomplish. Thus trust is built.

Giving each other space in a home is a wonderful gift to each other. Allowing for different preferences is a kindness one can bestow. Don't expect the next person to be perfect, but be careful to see the heart. Expressing appreciation as well as having an openly loving bond, nourishes a relationship like fertilizer and sunshine.

Have you married a person who promised to be true to you till death do you part, promised to treat you with kindness and love all the days of their life but went back on their promise? We all go back on this promise at times, but is this someone who continuously does the opposite of what anyone who loved and married would do?

There are some marriages where one person thinks they need to have the upper hand all the time and use criticisms and put-downs to achieve their desired goal of complete control. These are abusive marriages, and they will never work.

They may be nice for a while, just long enough for you to hope that all will be well, and then at just the opportune time, they push you off your happy hopeful place. You live in constant fear of them and do all they demand of you.

Eventually, you are like a plant that might be alive but only barely. You have no strength to stand up straight, never mind bloom. So your life continues as you receive just enough sunlight and drips of water to not die.

These plants need someone to notice their predicament and come to their rescue. God is our great lover, and He will nourish and care for us and heal us and even transplant us if necessary. All we need to do is believe on Him every day. Talk to Him. Cry to Him. He cares for the broken-hearted and will not discard you no matter where you are in life.

Matthew 12:20 describes His kind of love. "A bruised reed shall he not break, and smoking flax shall he not quench, till he send forth judgment unto victory."

# Turn On the Light

> "Darkness cannot understand the light.
> It cannot comprehend it."
> John 1:5

When you turn on the light, the darkness must flee. It's just a fact we take for granted. There just isn't room for both at the same place. The tiniest of lights dispels darkness.

A controller chooses to live without any consideration of what others might think or feel; they cannot comprehend a better way than their own. They don't recognize or have an awareness that what another might think is valid or even better than their own thinking. This is a sick way to be and part of the sickness is that the controller can't comprehend that they could be wrong.

"Turn on the light in your brain!" you want to tell them. Can anyone be narrower than to think theirs is the only right way, even when it doesn't make sense?

The controller thinks much like the person who still believes the earth is flat even though for hundreds of years we have known differently. What do you do with a person who stubbornly believes the earth is flat? You are nice to them and smile and nod and buy him lunch and ignore the silliness. You may not want them as your best friend but you smile and nod when you pass them on the street.

What do you do when you are married to one of these beings, and they demand you obey all their crazy concocted rules?

You can laugh and develop a clever sense of humor. You can live with them and become creative. You can live with them and endure. You can block out what they say, fog it out, turn all their words into a vapor that floats away. You can pretend you are in labor and having a baby. Learn to do the breathing exercises that mothers in labor use in order to distract themselves from the pain. You can choose to live as if they are right even though you know this is all wrong. You can do this just to keep the peace. But soon you will find out that in living a lie there is never any end of it and certainly no peace.

Light and darkness do not mix, and as long as there is strife between the two there will never be peace. Each person decides for him or herself what they will do in such a difficult situation. God sees dark as if it were light, He will hold your hand throughout any decision you make to free yourself from such a snare.

Keep your eyes on the Light of Jesus Christ and you will find your way to freedom.

> *"And have no fellowship with the unfruitful works of darkness, but rather reprove them." Ephesians 5:11*

# Forgiveness

Having to forgive someone means someone has done you wrong.

Forgiving is not overlooking the wrong. It is not ignoring the wrong. Nor is it denying the wrong. Christ never ignored our sin nor did he turn a blind eye. He paid the price, our price, for what we did. He would not have done that had He not fully acknowledged our sins and then felt the pain of sin.

The shedding of blood, and giving His life, showed He fully understood what our sin deserved. So in order to forgive someone of their sin, their sin must be acknowledged. Ask God to help you to forgive.

Your prayer could go something like this: "Dear Father in Heaven, Jack has wronged me, and I feel sad and angry, discouraged, miserable (whatever it is you feel).Thank you for dying on the cross for my sins and those of the whole world, including those of Jack. Please help me to forgive him, because I can't do it on my own. Please show me how to live with someone who hurts me purposely. Amen." Your job is to believe God will help you. God's job is to help you.

## Forgiveness is a big topic for a victim of abuse.

Forgiveness is a big topic for a victim of abuse. Many questions come to mind. How do I forgive someone who blindsides me, who has more tricks up their sleeve than you can count, who is a shark, gets you from behind? Who makes wrong look right and right wrong?

How does one forgive when the wrongs keep happening every day till you feel you're going crazy? Can you forgive and then un-forgive? How did Jesus forgive such people? Do I forgive only when they are sorry? How can I even want to forgive?

Forgiving does not mean trusting. If someone keeps repeating the same offences you will quite naturally move away from them. If someone harasses you, and hurts you, you might in time forgive them, but you will never want to be near them again. You may warn people about them. You may pray for them. But, unless they show true repentance and you can see their lives have had a turnaround, you won't even dream of trusting them again.

Jesus died for our sins and for our forgiveness, but He won't force this gift on us. We may do our part and forgive someone but it takes two to form a good relationship.

_____

_____

_____

_____

_____

_____

_____

_____

# What Is Your Quest?

"For with God nothing shall be impossible."
Luke 1:37

What is the one great quest in your life? Where do your adventures take you? What things occupy your time and your mind?

When you are young, your dream of 'adventurous expeditions' might occupy your mind day and night. As you become older and attempt to follow some of these quests, you might discover it is not quite as easy as you had anticipated. Money, family, responsibilities get in the way of doing all that you once dreamed of.

Whether you had a great and marvelous mission to pursue or simply wanted to have a happy home and family, obstacles coming your way can derail you time and time again, and sometimes hope is lost in the shuffle. Sometimes it is a disability, sometimes a disaster that hits unexpectedly, sometimes the person you married has no concept of what your dreams mean to you and may have no intention of trying to work things out between you.

If you have married an abuser, this impossibility of ever achieving your dream can bring on feelings of hopelessness and even despair. You have been put in a place where the only quest you have room for is the quest to do exactly what your spouse says to do every minute of every single day. They even speak for you and might say things like, "Ted likes to serve everyone" or "Ted likes to run little errands for me all day long" and "Ted looks forward to shopping for groceries every week" or answer to, "Am I not right, Ted?" And Ted nods his head obediently. He knows much better than to disagree. His whole life is given to obediently serving his controlling wife, and he nods and smiles at each request.

### Give it all – problems, discouragements, despair, depression, guilt and shame – to God.

Whatever it is that has caused your dream to disappear and has caused you to wonder at a much later stage in life whether there is anything of purpose and value left for you, it is not too late to dream again. It's really very simple. Give it all – problems, discouragements, despair, depression, guilt and shame – to God. How does one do this? Keeping it simple with God is the first step.

Simple words are usually closest to the truth. That goes for hearing God too. The first and simplest answer is usually from God. He not only gives new quests but he can bring old dreams back to life. It may not look exactly like you thought it should but don't be closed-minded when it comes to God. He has such a broad perspective; we may not always see where He is taking us. There are many stories in the Bible about God doing what man found completely impossible. The story of Elizabeth and Zachariah is found in Luke 1:5–25. They were the elderly parents of John the Baptist. He was the forerunner of Jesus' coming to earth. There are many such stories in the Bible to show us that with God, all things are possible.

_____

_____

_____

_____

# What is the Truth?

"Without understanding, covenant breakers,
without natural affection, implacable, unmerciful:"
Romans 1:31

Telling the truth is always the simpler route unless you live with an abuser. You can explain the truth to them in ten different ways, but they will still be able to prove you wrong. Explaining your point of view to them is exhausting and completely futile.

What truth do you want to hear? The bad truth or the good truth? The whole truth and nothing but the truth? It has been said that there are many different sides to every story. Which side is the closest to the truth?

The Chief Priests and Elders (who persuaded the multitude) did not care whether Jesus was innocent or not; they were determined to have him killed. They cared so little about the truth and were so determined to have their own way they made a fatal statement: "Then answered all the people and said, His blood be on us, and on our children. Then released he Barabbas unto them: and when he had scourged Jesus, he delivered him to be crucified." Matthew 27: 20, 25

It is a sad thing to fall into the hands of one who pretends they are good but act so only to gain control. It is even more tragic to be the one who does the controlling.

Controllers are very lonely people. They may work day and night to look the part of a perfect person (their version of perfect) and control those closest to them to do the same. They can be very cruel in the process and have no idea how to truly love. How to be vulnerable and real. Nobody wants to be around them. They set themselves up to be detested. Just to keep them from having angry outbursts, some will appear to like them or some may feel sorry for them but nobody really wants to be around controllers. Not even their 'nice' can be trusted because everything they do, nice or not, is for their own benefit and selfish gain.

What does one do then with these people? If I'm nice to them and want to show them a better way, they just see that as a chance to walk all over you. You will end up being a martyr with no rewards or benefit to either of you.

**You may need to decide when it is time to walk away.**

This would be a good time to remember to walk your own walk. You may pray for the abuser. You may pray for wisdom. You will want to keep your head about you, whether you decide to make some blunt statements or remain quietly polite. You may need to decide when it is time to walk away. Don't let your heart be contaminated with anger and revenge. These controllers are to be pitied more than you. Just remember no one can answer for us or for them, and only God can discern the heart.

_____

_____

_____

_____

_____

# A Power Imbalance

How does a power imbalance happen?

A person might invite an imbalance by voluntarily giving up power. Playing the disabled person is another way to give up power. Choosing to do a job poorly invites the other person to pick up the slack. You gain one kind of power when you give up another. To be too helpful could invite an imbalance. To be too fussy about how things must be done also creates inequality. Sometimes there is disagreement on what is an equal share of power. Sometimes there is an imbalance out of necessity.

Too much power at the top causes apathy in the workplace. Not enough power causes frustration.

The Pharisees in the Bible were the Jewish law keepers and held the offices of power. They knew the law and kept it religiously and demanded it of the people. As ironical as it may seem, the law blinded them to the truth. Some, even though knowing the truth, chose to operate in deception in order to hold on to this power.

Jesus, on the other hand, though He was God, came as a humble man to this earth. He always had the power but kept it under control, choosing the humble seat, to the point of giving His life on the cross for the sins of mankind.

**You may not be able to rectify the problem but one thing you can do is KNOW where the real problem lies.**

Nobody can better judge whether in your relationship there is an imbalance, than yourself. The only problem is in an abusive situation, the abuser will disagree even if it stares them in the face. This is because a controller loves power too much. You must stand alone and be strong.

You may not be able to rectify the problem but one thing you can do is KNOW where the real problem lies. That alone will give you strength, even though it is as if you are imprisoned and muzzled. Know that the truth is always a step toward freedom. In truth you can take many steps. Yes, it may be slow progress, but keeping to the truth will in the end set you free.

Seek the truth. Cling to the truth. Love the truth. Live by the truth. Even when you do not look for a fight, in an abusive house, truth telling will cause turmoil. But remember, even just KNOWING the truth, it WILL set you free.

> *"And ye shall know the truth, and the truth shall make you free." John 8:32*

_____

_____

_____

_____

_____

_____

## What Makes You Tick?

> "In the history of science, the clockwork
> universe compares the universe to a
> mechanical clock. It continues ticking along,
> as a perfect machine, with its gears
> governed by the laws of physics, making every
> aspect of the machine predictable."
> —Wikipedia, *Clockwork Universe*

When something works like clockwork it works with precision. It is considered to be reliable.

We each are created with our own clockwork. What is it that makes you tick? This is a question sometimes asked when we want to know what excites you, what is your passion, what makes you come alive. God knows everything about each of our clockworks because he created us.

Sometimes our internal clockwork gets broken.

Abusers like to tamper with our clockwork. They like to readjust who we are to suit themselves. They use every trick in the book to make and create this person they think would be a perfect life partner.

A lump of clay is good for shaping. They choose a person that is easygoing and wants to please. This way, they envision molding and shaping their partner just the way they want. What they don't know is that, what God made cannot be improved upon. Their spouse was perfectly created from the beginning.

So God created man in his own image, in the image of God created He him; male and female created He them ... And God saw every thing that He had made, and, behold, it was very good. And the evening and the morning were the sixth day. Genesis 1:27,31

Then mankind decided to sin.

This world is governed by sin due to a decision 'man' made in the Garden of Eden. Now we are in a broken world, and it takes much hard work to live peacefully. There are many different things people do to try to make it better here. Some of these efforts might seem to work for a while but none work very well at all. Even the good efforts are merely temporary fixes. The abuser has the mindset that they can fix his or her spouse. This only shows how broken they themselves are. Fixing someone else is not the solution.

**Read the Bible and don't make it complicated.**

It makes sense that if one needs fixing we go to the clock maker. The Creator, God, our Heavenly Father is our clock maker. His Book the Bible is the 'fix it' manual. It is as simple as it sounds. Read the Bible and don't make it complicated. You won't understand every-thing but listen to what you do understand. That is how a relationship is built with your clock maker. You learn the language of your Maker and soon you will understand many things about how to live a life here in this broken world; the real life that you were intended to have. No two people are alike so don't copy anyone.

"O Lord, thou hast searched me, and known me. Thou knowest my downsitting and mine uprising, thou understandest my thought afar off. Thou compassest my path and my lying down, and art acquainted with all my ways. For there is not a word in my tongue, but, lo, O Lord, thou knowest it altogether. Thou hast beset me behind and before, and laid thine hand upon me. Such knowledge is too wonder-ful for me; it is high, I cannot attain unto it." Psalm 139:1–6

## What are the Real Triggers?

"Do not envy a man of violence
And do not choose any of his ways."
Proverbs 3:31

What are the real reasons for the abuse? Can we predict when these outbursts will happen?

It is a known fact that a new baby in the family triggers it. Moving to a different house, or town, can cause multiple outbursts until the family has settled into their new place. Holiday celebrations can cause accelerated violence. Just before guests come to visit or after they leave can be red flags.

What abusers fear most is losing control. Uncertain situations like a new baby or guests in the home can make them feel that they are losing the 'front and center seat of power'. Sometimes the outburst is completely unpredictable. The violence just suddenly happens. Whatever the given reason that presents itself at that moment, it will do for a violent outburst. It may just be a wife a little too happy, that can make him feel unsure and need an altercation.

There is a definite insecurity in these savage eruptions. What a huge insecurity it would have to be, to have such a bullish outbreak as to hit and physically hurt ones closest to you – even your pregnant wife, or your little innocent child, never mind cats and dogs – to get back their balance of control. The chronic abuser may do his or her evil with crafty ease, and administer torment with a smirk on their face. They may have the choicest of words and be very smooth. The intent is still to suppress in order to elevate themselves.

What they fear most is losing control. When you don't do as they say, they act as though you are cutting off their airways. Although that is true, still that is not the real reason for the abuse. They have made the choice at one point in their life that they will abuse so that is what they do.

"The violence of the wicked will drag them away, Because they refuse to act with justice." Proverbs 21:7

Isaiah 59:1–8 has a Biblical description of a violent person.

_____

_____

_____

_____

_____

_____

_____

_____

_____

## "He Will"

"He who dwells in the secret place of the Most High
Shall abide under the shadow of the Almighty."
Psalm 91:1

A comforting song by Jim Reeves, "He Will"

"He will open up the doorway you never knew was there
He will show you many things you knew not how
He will let you know he listens to your every prayer
He will save you by the mercy of His love."

How does one turn it all over to Jesus when you live in constant mental torture? You know there will be more the next day and the next and the next. How do you turn it all over to Jesus?

When you're in the middle of a horrendous experience nothing will seem to help. Later you might even see some good in it all, but in the moment, nothing is good or bearable.

Day after day, you fear the person who shares a house and life with you. You sit at the same table, go to church together, go to bed together. Your whole mind is preoccupied with getting it right so there will be no angry outbursts or constant orders, long lectures, and detailed criticisms. When there is ever any quiet time, all you want to do is escape and rest your head.

All your work feels like pushing a rock uphill. You want to keep the peace at all cost, and the cost is very high.

Stop and look at it this way. You are doing what is right and good. You are doing the best you can under the circumstances. What you do will make a difference in ways you won't expect. Look at it like you are going to university and every day what you learn will be credited to you for some PhD degree. You aren't there yet. In fact, you might have two or seven years left in this degree. One assignment doesn't seem like much progress, but each assignment well done gives you credits toward your final success. And in your case, the assignments are much harder than assignments in a university.

A plaque to be hung on the wall of your accomplishments will never be given to you. You won't see your name in the paper listing all your accomplishments. A 'well done' may not come from many people but it is important that you see what you have accomplished; what you have been through; what you have learned. The 'WELL DONE' is not at all about how well you pleased the abuser. It might be how well you did it in spite of the pressure and criticisms. It might be how well you kept your sanity intact. It might be a 'well done' for God who kept you together in one piece. A well done might not be that the abuser is kept happy, but that you are somehow able to keep yourself happy.

You will have such a strong sense that you know what you have come through that you will need no plaque. You might have spent so much time serving an ungrateful mean person for so long, you finally graduated from your very special type of education. You could say you have earned your PhD in S.H.I.T. You'll be an expert in manure. You'll be able to smell it from miles away and warn everyone about what's ahead if they keep going that way.

Once you've been through it and come out the other side you will see what a difference your prayers and efforts have made.

You might not know how to give it all over to Jesus, but say the words anyway, "I give this all to you, Jesus." You may or may not know it but He will be carrying you. Sometimes you will be given nuggets of enlightenments. You may not be able to read scripture or pray. In these times, know that one verse read is an accomplishment. Know that your moaning and groaning are prayers. Your tears are prayers. Even your angry outbursts are heard and God understands the heart of the matter. He will bring you through.

> *"I will instruct thee and teach thee in the way which thou shalt go; I will guide thee with mine eye." Psalm 32:8*

_____

_____

_____

_____

_____

_____

_____

_____

# Different Kinds of Abuse

There are different kinds of abuse and some of them are harder to detect than others. There are also different degrees of abuse.

Some abusers are like snakes slithering around in frightfully quiet ways and others come in as roaring lions. Some are like bulls in china shops and some are sly foxes, while still others are like laughing hyenas, using sick humor or sarcasm meant to hurt, to bring you down or make you feel stupid and worthless.

Whether your abuser has the look of a snake, lion, bull, fox or hyena, they all play with their victims, overpowering them and hurting them.

Some abuses are harder to detect than others. Some play the sick or helpless game where anyone with a sensitive and kind heart will get sucked in. Continuous complaining may get the pastor's, counselor's and caregiver's attention. Purposely doing a poor job so someone else will pick up the slack is a form of abuse. Some can stare you down with an evil eye, and no words need be spoken.

There are always those abuses that are unintentional, and the abuser is so wrapped up in their controlling thoughts that they don't know the damage they are doing. Self abuse comes in many shapes and sizes. You may treat yourself poorly because of laziness, depression, hopelessness or addictive cravings. Some may want something so badly that they sacrifice everything of true value like time, money, relationships and family, in order to get that larger house or fancier car.

Nice abuse can happen where someone is so nice to you that you can't say no to what they want of you. Guilt usually is mixed in with what this person has come to expect of you. Religious abuse is using religion to control and give direction to another person. It can be done nicely or not so nicely.

## In some cases, law enforcement may be necessary to keep the abuser at bay.

You cannot fight abuse with abuse. You cannot fight it with trickery or game playing or humor. You will get nowhere with reasoning or debate or even with an intellectual mind. The best way to fight abuse is to make short of it. Don't stand and listen to the shenanigans because it is meant to suck you in. State your case and move on. Leave the room. Find excuses to go somewhere. Some will follow you to the ends of the earth so you will need to be shrewd and sly, clever and unfrazzled at all times. Of course this is quite impossible, and in some cases, law enforcement may be necessary to keep the abuser at bay. Abuse comes by way of an evil spirit. It is a spirit that does not want to listen and understand another person. They want to get along only on their own terms. No negotiations will ever break through the thick veneer.

"But now I have written unto you not to keep company, if any man that is called a brother be a fornicator, or covetous, or an idolater, or a railer,(a verbal abuser) or a drunkard, or an extortioner; with such an one no not to eat." 1 Corinthians 5:11

# A Stony Path

> "Each of us may be sure that if God sends us on stony paths;
> He will provide us with strong shoes,
> and He will not send us out on any journey
> for which He does not equip us well."
> —Alexander Maclaren

"And thine ears shall hear a word behind thee, saying, This is the way, walk ye in it, when ye turn to the right hand, and when ye turn to the left." Isaiah 30:21

In an abusive situation, so much can happen that is confusing. The biggest issue a victim of abuse has is to be continually misunderstood and misinterpreted. First you hear contradictory statements that are proven correct. Then you say truths as true as can be, and they are misunderstood and proven incorrect. Actions are also confusing. One day they are sugary sweet, and the next day an evil shadow falls over them and the very steps they take are frightening.

Know that these are the stony paths. The days of walking on rough terrain. Listen carefully on these days or years, to your Heavenly Maker. Your abuser might think they have you pinned, but they are wrong. You might look like you are beaten down, but you will not stay down.

"We are troubled on every side, yet not distressed; we are perplexed, but not in despair; ... Persecuted, but not forsaken; cast down, but not destroyed; ... that the life also of Jesus might be made manifest in our body." 2 Corinthians 4:8,9,10

Most victims of abuse do not believe they are strong and can stand on their own two feet. They downplay all their accomplishments and even resort to giving their abuser credit for every achievement.

There was a woman, abused throughout her many years of marriage. She made her way through the abuse in stages. First she was in shock and blamed everything on herself. Then she became sad and depressed, holding on desperately and blindly to the marriage and to raising her children. She was like a person flailing for breath while pretending that everything was okay. It was a complete stupidity how she falsely thought somehow she was to blame for all of this. After many years of gasping for air she began to see past the shock of it. She began her quest of learning. If only she had gone for help, she laments now, the process would have been much faster. So she learned; even while staggering through the muck; even while continuing to heed every request and demand from her abuser. She was still playing dodgeball with the abuser rather than go head on and deal with it. Yet she was determined to learn.

After a while, her learning picked up speed, as she became less and less afraid of the abuser's outbursts. Where before she was ashamed of her panic attacks, she began not to care. She'd have bursts of outrage, but it wasn't the end.

She continued to read and started to talk more to friends.

Finally, she was learning how to go on the Internet and chat with others who were in a similar situation.

Though she was becoming stronger she began to think it was too late. She was getting old now, and had learned much about how to live with abuse. "My best years, my youth, is gone," she lamented, "I might as well ride it out now." And besides, there was so much she would have to learn should she go now and live on her own.

The Lord had other plans. Just as it was not too late to save Lazarus; even after he was dead Jesus came at just the right time to raise him from the dead. Just like Lazarus, it was not too late to rescue this woman. He still had a plan for her even though she no longer had her youth. He came with a new occupation that was perhaps the bigger calling. Her stony path may well be her readying for her new line of work.

_____

_____

_____

_____

_____

_____

_____

_____

_____

_____

_____

_____

_____

# Free from Condemnation

Those living with abuse often feel condemned all day long. All day they worry about making mistakes. Big ones, little ones, stupid ones, dreamed up ones ... They live all their days hoping for some freedom and peace from these condemning voices.

The following statement was written by a woman who was wonderfully set free from rules and regulations, do's and don'ts and from condemnation, when she escaped an abusive partner.

"To me, making a mistake means I'm free. It means I'm alive. It means I am real and can think. Making a mistake means I did something! It also means I'm learning. It means I made a decision! Making a mistake means I'm more than passive. It means I beat my fears. What a THING – to be FREE TO MAKE MISTAKES." —T. Louise.

When you live a long time with an abuser who demands and criticizes, gives orders and explains everything to death about all the why's they are always right, you learn to sleep and breathe what the abuser says. You really forget all that was ever inside your own head in exchange for what the abuser thinks. Your goal becomes to read the abuser's mind so completely that they no longer need to give you orders. To be a step ahead of the abuser in order to avoid the blow-ups. Anything short of that is failing.

But they always find a reason to criticize. They can put up a bigger fuss over nothing, than Mount St. Helens did when she blew her top. There is no time to think, just to run for cover. When they catch up to you they will talk your head off with lectures, and you will have no reprieve. If you run to the other room or to the bathroom, or leave the house they follow you. And keep talking. If they ever leave the house and there be some peace, all you want to do is sleep. Certainly all your thinking ability is gone.

They are expert on everything, even things they have never themselves done. Their word is the law, and they want you afraid of it.

When T. Louise finally left the abusive situation air filled her lungs. Her brain began to function again. All her wheels began to turn. She could make decisions and learned many things. Condemnation had held her down and shut her mind and body but now she was free, even to make mistakes. Colossians 2:16–23

---

---

---

---

---

---

---

---

# Setting Your Compass

Do you have a trusty compass you can rely on when you go through the confusions of life? Do you have someone whom you trust and hold on to, in spite of anything that might happen to you? Do you trust your own instincts and senses?

Always make sure you are not below your situation, being squashed into hopelessness. Rise up higher to be on the upper side of things. If you have a trusty compass in a deep dark forest it will help you greatly in finding your way out. You may be in fear of the unknown pitfalls, but as long as your eyes are on the compass you can hope to reach safety.

**No matter how right your abuser
sounds, they can't be trusted.**

There are truths you can hold on to that will help you through an unknown, and frightening place in life. These truths will help you not to get crushed below your circumstances. One general truth is that no matter how right your abuser sounds, they can't be trusted. Their angry outbursts and criticisms are never accurate. Validate your own thoughts and feelings above what people say.

We all make mistakes. Don't blow that fact up to mean that you committed the unpardonable sin. There is a right and wrong way on how to do things but these are not laws and sometimes they differ between people. We all get devastated – sometimes due to our own doings. Don't let it crush you but get over the devastation and forgive yourself.

# A Soul that Pants

"As the hart panteth after the water brooks,
so panteth my soul after thee, O God.
My soul thirsteth for God, for the living God:"
Psalm 42:1–2a

We need water every day, and our bodies get very thirsty, eventually leading to death if we don't get it.

Water brooks sound so delicious. Be it a trickling stream or a rushing river, even the sound of it refreshes us. Water washes clean, and uplifts us and makes us happy. It is invigorating, stimulating; it is Life!

It is a good thing to thirst after God ... 'for you shall be filled'. Matthew 5:6

With our carnal minds we cannot understand scripture and it will not satisfy "Because the carnal mind is enmity against God: for it is not subject to the law of God, neither indeed can be." Romans 8:7. Our own goodness is as filthy rags. We need illumination from the Lord to understand the things of the Lord.

If one tries to make sense of scripture with our own minds we might see much good in it, but the soul satisfying elements will not be there. There could be the value of its poetry or the documentation of its history, maybe the value of a good lesson learned, but with our human minds we will not taste it as one does a satisfying drink from a well.

Our carnal minds are capable of twisting scripture, misinterpreting it to mean what we want it to mean or to use it to manipulate people to do what we want them to do. When scripture is misinterpreted it gives no satisfaction. It can be used to coerce saying, "thus saith the Lord" when he saith nothing like that. Some abusers are very fluent in Bible knowledge to make you do what they want. They act like they are an authority but nothing they quote from scripture ever satisfies. It only condemns. Even Satan uses scripture, which he did when he tempted Jesus.

Have you ever sat in church and heard such a sermon where no scripture is used? To say it is frustrating and extremely disappointing is putting it lightly. When we are hungry and thirsty we come to the table expecting to be satisfied, and that is an excellent way to approach the reading of scripture.

Jeremiah 15:16 says, "Thy words were found, and I did eat them; and thy word was unto me the joy and rejoicing of mine heart." 1 Corinthians 2:6–16 explains very well how the Holy Spirit reveals to us the things of God; "Things that no 'man' knows."

When someone holds scripture over your head to condemn you, don't listen to it. When your own voice inside of you condemn you; know that it is from Satan the Devil.

The Lord Jesus Christ; He will hear us and illuminate to us truths that will fill and satisfy us. Like water every day, we need His Word to satisfy the thirst, which He will gladly fill.

> "Let us draw near with a true heart in full assurance of faith, having our hearts sprinkled from an evil conscience, and our bodies washed with pure water."
> Hebrews 10:22

A Soul that Pants

# A Still Small Voice

"And he said, Go forth, and stand upon the mount before
the LORD. And, behold the LORD passed by, and a great
and strong wind rent the mountains, and brake in pieces the
rocks before the LORD: but the LORD was not in the wind:
and after the wind an earthquake; but the LORD was not in
the earthquake and after the earthquake a fire; but the LORD
was not in the fire: and after the fire a still small voice."
1 Kings 19:11

You might have heard for yourself, that 'still small voice' from heaven,
which may have been just a few basic words simply spoken. It likely
was the first thing you heard when you questioned to the Lord. It
might even have come before you finished asking. It is almost laugh-
able how very simply the Lord answers.

When you're accustomed to listening to the loud yells or strong
opinions of an abuser it becomes hard to listen to the kind and gentle
voice of The God who leads us without pushing or shoving. The per-
sistence of a controller can easily drown out our own thoughts and
also the still small voice within us.

Whether your controlling person in your life is your spouse or
another person, find ways to take a break away from them whenever
you can. At this time away, aim to get yourself on level ground with
your own thoughts and the still small voice inside you. It is important

to put away all fear of the abuser. Picture them to be a paper lion. They are only as powerful as you are afraid of them.

## When abusers appear powerful they are actually showing their greatest fears.

When abusers appear powerful they are actually showing their greatest fears. When they seem most confident they are actually terribly anxious. When they are most controlling, they are really most insecure. If you are ever foolish enough to confront them with this they will rip strips off you, you didn't know you had. Just know in your heart of hearts that they are acting out of terror and trepidation.

Best for the abuser is that you stay calm, quiet, peaceful, composed, serene, diplomatic, unruffled, and basically show no emotions. This may be quite impossible when someone is raging at you and won't stop, but you can always practice. It has been known to work to quiet a fierce altercation by lowering your voice to a whisper and say over and over, "Okay, okay, okay, okay. I won't do that again. I'll behave." And so on. And so on. Sarcasm aside, the still small voice of the Creator of the Universe, the Lover of our souls, the Great Shepherd that lay down His life for the sheep; learn His gentle voice and listen to His simple yet profound instructions to your day by day trials. Maybe tomorrow, maybe down the road a bit, He will help you out of your situation. In the meantime, He will give you some awesome wisdom to help you through.

---

---

---

---

# Create in Me a Clean Heart

"Create in me a clean heart, oh Lord,
renew a right spirit within me."
Psalm 51:10

The prayer that continues goes something like this: "Do not turn your back on me, Oh Lord. Give me back the joy that is beyond comprehension and give me daily strength. If you do this I will tell those who don't know you about you so that those looking for you will turn to you. Deliver me from (this abuse) and I will sing aloud of your righteousness. O Lord, open my lips and my mouth to praise you. You do not look for sacrifice but rather ... an honest and humble heart."

"The sacrifices of God are a broken spirit: a broken and a contrite heart, O God, thou wilt not despise." Psalm 51:17

It's not all the do's and don'ts that the Lord is looking for. It is the heart that He wants. Someone might make mistakes but when you know that they have a good heart you know that they did not mean to hurt you. We all hurt each other sometimes, mostly unknowingly; but you know pretty well whether that person's heart is good or not. If indeed it is, it is so much easier to deal with the mistake.

God knows our hearts even though we make mistakes.

Abusers criticize, even when they can see that their spouse has done nothing wrong. They may even have gone far above and beyond a reasonable effort to please, yet the abuser feels the need to find fault. Nothing is good enough for them, and they expect even things they themselves could never carry out. A victim of abuse often continues to blame themselves after they have done their best.

After Jesus died on the cross and paid for our sins, we who believe in Him have become free from the law. This is a concept an abuser does not understand. They continue to push the law on their victim as if that is how we become acceptable before God and man.

It is a most wonderful faith walk to know we are not under the law anymore. The devil hates this and so does the controlling person. Abusers often like to dangle our so-called wrong doings in front of us. It is very hard to cope with such abuse and to hang on to what is true, and that is that we are forgiven and righteous before God.

**Hold on tight to the truth that you are guilt-free.**

When these hard times are upon you, hold on tight to the truth that you are guilt-free. The problem belongs to the faultfinder. It is better that you are in good standing with the God of the universe than with any human being, even a controlling and abusive faultfinder.

_____

_____

_____

_____

_____

_____

_____

## Creating an Ambience

We all create a certain ambiance in our home just by who we are. Do you like a home warm and informal or do you like more formality? The type of lighting you use, the music in the background, the scents in the air, plants and planters around the room, whether your place has friendly clutter or is warm and tidy, all point to the ambiance we have created for ourselves to be comfortable in.

Part of caring for yourself is creating a place to live in that you are easy with. Your home should be a place where you can let down your guard, put your feet up and do those things you find relaxing. You also want to be able to work in a safe and comfortably organized fashion.

Everything you choose to do can be done in a good spirit. Some of us live in a small space, maybe we don't have the luxuries some can afford but we still create a certain atmosphere whether we know it or not. Our very moods create certain impressions in our home.

Who we are, what we believe in, what our heritage is, our history, the circumstances we are in will all in some way or another be evident in our dwelling places.

If you are living with an agitated controller, they might have a huge say in how they want or don't want their house to look. Their priority might not be to be comfortable or to let their hair down. You might have to work around clinical perfectionism, or a sterilized atmosphere of coldness to create something slightly peaceful.

King Saul in the Bible was Israel's first king. He did well until he thought he knew better than God. He disobeyed some crucial instructions among a string of other proud rebellions. Finally, God was fed up with him and removed the Holy spirit from him. Saul became increasingly agitated by waves of madness.

David was called to play the harp for the king to sooth his spirit. It was like a cat and mouse situation where on one hand it soothed King Saul and on the other hand the king was jealous and was continually after David to kill him. It was much like how abusive relationships work. You come when called, do what you are told to do, but the appreciation is short-lived.

David created an ambience of peace for Saul, who was temporarily pacified, until God saw fit to remove Saul from the scene and David fulfilled his calling and became the next king.

While we are in a difficult situation, all we may be able to do is ask God how we can create an ambience of peace around us. We may live for a time to appease the abuser and to give ourselves and our children a measure of peace. As you rely on Jesus daily, for all your large and small needs, He will reveal to you when the time has come to be set free. It may come sooner than you think.

"... the Lord saved them (Israel) by a great deliverance." 1 Chronicles 11:14

"Wherefore gird up the loins of your mind, be sober, and hope to the end for the grace that is to be brought unto you at the revelation of Jesus Christ;" 1 Peter 1:13

_____

_____

_____

_____

# Do What You Can

> "Know ye not that ye are the temple of God,
> and that the Spirit of God dwelleth in you?
> If any man defile the temple of God, them shall God destroy:
> for the temple of God is holy, which temple ye are."
> 1 Corinthians 3:16–17

Are you treating your body and mind with respect and care? Do you listen to your own mind, or do you ignore what you think is right?

Most victims of abuse cover for their abuser because of their fear of the impending violence and the intense manipulation if they don't. Do you coddle and feel sorry for the abuser saying they can't help themselves?

There are things you can do that would help the situation.

Of course you will receive much opposition from your abuser if you disclose to them your thoughts and plans, so keep it close to your heart and go about your business as usual, with a few exceptions.

- Read up on what it is to be abused.
- Take care of yourself. Never say you can't. You can learn how.
- Believe there are answers and be determined to find them.
- This is not a time to nurse your victim mentality.
- This is not the time to feel sorry for your abuser.
- Practice being calm – calm and decisive. When you practice, don't expect perfection; it's a practice.

- You MUST find help. You cannot do it by yourself. Don't play tough. These situations are the meanest most difficult of any relationship problems.
- Don't listen to the controller's tears or their nice. They'll turn and bite you in the butt if you do.
- Don't tell your abuser anything that is in your heart. Learn to show no emotions.
- Plan ways to escape safely. Don't look back.
- Your abuser is NOT your friend.
- Only God can help the abuser. Staying with this person could be standing in the way of what God wants to do in their life.

Make your own list of what you can do to change your very tough situation. The important thing is to do what you can even if they are small steps.

_____

_____

_____

_____

_____

_____

_____

_____

## Cry Aloud

"Cry aloud, spare not; Lift up thy voice like a trumpet,
and show my people their transgressions,
and the house of Jacob their sins."
Isaiah 58:1

"For they bind heavy burdens and grievous to be borne
and lay them on men's shoulders;
but they themselves will not move them with one of their fingers."
Matthew23:4

Those who are abused do not always know that the treatment they are receiving is completely wrong and evil. They might think they are bad and deserve to be hurt and punished.

They may never have heard of abuse and perhaps think they deserve this kind of treatment. They might so desperately want a good marriage that they deny anything is wrong. They may have accepted and believed the abusive words. They might even feel sorry for the abuser for having to put up with someone like themselves.

**Nobody deserves to be treated with abuse.**

This is dangerous thinking because nobody deserves to be treated with abuse. Not even animals deserve such treatment. If you think you deserve this, your thinking is already screwed up. Also, to put up with such treatment tells the person who rules over you that it is okay to treat you this way. If you make no objections they will never stop. It is a serious sickness, but they will never overcome it on their own. It is sad to say but the abuser will not change easily and if they are encouraged to stay abusive, there is no hope for them at all. The most devastating symptom of their sickness is that they don't see the seriousness of their condition. If you wanted a nice loving peaceful relationship, you are out of luck – it won't happen. It is a big hard pill to swallow but the sooner you accept it the sooner you can find the best way to deal with your particular situation.

Chronic abusive controllers do not listen to reason but will use it against you if you try to explain it to them. They may give the appearance of hearing you but they just get better and better at talking in circles and taunting you into thinking that this time it will be different.

Start by telling yourself the truth. You do not deserve to be misunderstood or bossed around or disrespected in any way. Then find ways to take care of yourself. Listen to your head and your heart. Don't tell your abuser anything precious or significant because they will take it away from you. Realize that your relationship will never be normal. If you stay with this person you might become very good at coping but it can't ever be normal with such an imbalance of power.

If you don't have anyone you can trust then try to go online and search for a chat group you can join. Don't give up hope but search in every way you can think of, for help.

Search the scriptures for help from God, your Heavenly Father. Psalm 91:15 says, "He shall call upon me, and I will answer him: I will be with him in trouble, I will deliver him and honor him."

# Criminal and Devilish

How quickly Peter got sidetracked!

> "But he turned, and said unto Peter, Get thee behind me,
> Satan: thou art an offence unto me: for thou savourest not
> the things that be of God, but those that be of men."
> Matthew 16:23

Peter was a follower of Jesus; he walked and talked with Him every day. Can you imagine being a face to face student of the Son of God? The Father of the Universe? The Creator of all the stars? Peter walked and talked with this Jesus! Touched Him. Looked Him in the eye. Though Peter was just an unlearned fisherman, people could tell that he had been with Jesus.

What had Peter done that was so devilish as to be called, 'Satan'? If you read the passage you will see that Peter merely saw things from a human standpoint. That was his crime.

Controllers take a very strong standpoint. They treat their own selfish ways as though it were the way of God Almighty. Respect for another one's way of thinking is not even considered unless it is somehow to their advantage. They have become so fluent in their own thinking that they can make their way seem like the only right way. Such people can be incredibly convincing, but their way is carnal and devilish.

People stay for years with such abusive spouses. Children are raised by parents who control their every move. Staff in a workplace grit their teeth and stay working as they are abused by such a boss. These controllers live and breathe and are criminally smooth in their control and know just what strings to pull, what nice to be, what to say and not say to keep these people around, yanking their chains in just the right way every day to keep them on and torture them. They are criminals on the loose and know just how to manipulate their world and not be caught and labeled correctly.

Like Peter we all have devilish capabilities. He was not a criminal so to speak, but he was capable of relying on his own fleshly mind that seemed pure to him. Whether we just want to see things from OUR standpoint or are involved in the criminal activity of controlling others, it would be good to repent and turn from our wicked ways, and let God do the controlling in our lives.

# When There is Still a Little Bit More Work

"Then said they unto him, What shall we do,
that we might work the works of God?
Jesus answered and said unto them,
This is the work of God, that ye believe on him
whom he hath sent."
John 6:28–29

You may have been set free from your abuser and are doing everything possible to heal from a destructive relationship. You may have been to doctors and psychiatrists for assessment and the type of help they give. Maybe you have found a helpful support group, and have had counseling for the different abuses that have happened to you. Some people find the 'Divorce Care' program extremely helpful. Some move ahead almost without help. You are a brave soul, braver than most, if you have done this on your own! There is nothing easy about divorce settlements, and the cost is high financially, emotionally, and spiritually, in these times and a high cost to all involved.

"He giveth power to the faint; and to them that have no might he increaseth strength. Isaiah." 40:29

If you are in this place then give God all the glory. He wants to do even more for you than He has done, and if you stay close to Him through faith and trust, He will do more for you in your life than you can imagine. You may be doing a good job of getting by and making a new life for yourself but with God there is always more work. Not work on your part, but on His. He wants to bless you more. Heal you more. Help you recover far beyond what you ever dreamed or imagined. The only thing for you to do is to believe.

"Yes, Lord, I give my life to you to heal even more. I trust You with my life." That is when all the excitement starts. He might have something small for you to do, or very large, but He'll let you know, and He'll tell you how to do the work. He'll give you strength to do it, one step at a time. He'll figure out how He will help, you just need to trust. You'll never be sorry, and you will literally feel His warm smile on you as he watches you make progress.

Don't be afraid of making mistakes. He smiles at you even when you make mistakes because He can fix them. His greatest pleasure is to see you believe in Him. Daily mistakes don't bother Him when your eyes are on Him.

Maybe you have been extra sensitive due to your abuse and mistrust, and have told someone off and hurt them really badly. Relax! It's not the end of the world. God might want to teach you how to repent and show love after what you did. How much can that hurt? In this way, you are becoming whole and learning how to deal with tricky situations. Apologizing and forgiving are good things. It's a sign of the work God is doing in you and a sign of you becoming more and more healthy and mature.

"Being confident of this very thing, that He which hath begun a good work in you will perform it until the day of Jesus Christ." Philippians 1:6

_____

_____

_____

_____

# The Snowflakes

"And there are also many other things which Jesus did, the which,
if they should be written every one,
I suppose that even the world itself could not contain
the books that should be written. Amen."
John 21:25

"The Love of God is greater far, than any tongue or pen can tell."
—Old Hymn

God does not run out; He is never at His wits' end, and is never stuck. He always was, is, and always will be. It would be impossible to write it all down – what He does and who He is. No two snowflakes are the same and we all have our own very unique fingerprints. How can one comprehend it?

Oh, to have the wonderment of a child! Children have such faith and that is why they don't have the trouble many adults have in how to pray and in seeing God in real life situations. Maybe it is partly because they accept the fact that they are dependent and have not yet learned what it is to be too proud to ask for help. It would seem easy for a child to understand that if God can make each snowflake different from all the others, than He must have the power to help us in any situation.

We may be up against a wall with an abusive spouse. To stay with such a spouse is not unusual as many stay because they believe the lies the abuser tells them. They believe they can't take care of their children or themselves. They believe their spouse is smarter and stronger than they are and don't trust themselves. They may also believe that God will punish them if they leave their spouse.

The controlling spouse never seems to believe they will be punished for their own bad behavior and can even preach a pretty good sermon on topics like God hating divorce. God does hate divorce as He hates all sin and you might say, He hates the sin of violence, deception and pride. He declares that whoever discourages a young child, it would be better off they have a millstone hung around their necks and be drowned. Matthew 18:6

That God hates divorce does not mean you should stay with a person who abuses you. You probably hate divorce as much and have done everything to make the marriage work, and prayed all the prayers you can think of, for your abuser and for the abuse that is happening in your home. Sometimes it is not our fault, why some things just don't go right. If one chooses to ignore God's voice of warning, God may eventually turn His back on such a person and leave him or her to their own devices. Even as God does not force us to listen to Him, we cannot force an abuser to understand. Leaving a caustic marriage can be the best thing in a terrible situation – best for your sanity and best for your children.

The spouse who sees the abuse every day, sees how the children are affected and does nothing about it, is as much to blame for theirs and their child's troubles as the abuser is.

**Take steps to bring yourself and your children to safety.**

When taken before the law, such children can be removed from the home. You may feel helpless and weak, but Jesus is waiting for the helpless to come to Him! Let Him help you in your great time of need. Have the faith of a child when you come to Him. Many miracles and things Jesus did are recorded in the Bible, but also many are not written down. Let your miracle be one of these.

Call on Him and then take steps to bring yourself and your children to safety. God has promised: "He shall call upon me, and I will answer him: I will be with him in trouble; I will deliver him, and honour him." Psalm 91:15

God has as many ways to deliver you as there are snowflakes.

# Up and Out

Joy and sorrow often live side by side in us. Even at the most joyous times, there may be some sorrows in our lives.

Sometimes the joys have the upper hand and other times the sorrows do. When you go through grief or sickness, these want to take over and throw you overboard and drown you completely. Depression can be a downward spiral that is pure mental anguish. It can feel like it has a life of its own and won't let go.

When you live with someone who abuses you and works every day to keep a tight rein on you, till you can't breathe, you may not have time for depression or a nervous breakdown. These creatures have such a hold on their victims, it actually saves the victim the trouble of breaking down. You just become a walking talking zombie and you don't even bother thinking. When it has come to this, your situation is critical. If you are reading this and see yourself in such a situation, you can still wake up from your brainwashing. (Brainwashing causes you to doubt yourself and blindly trust the abuser.)

- First thing is to wake from your situation.
- Second is to stop hiding the truth and tell someone. Pride and fear must go!
- Accept the pain you are in; the discomfort, the awkwardness. Just carry through.
- Accept help. Don't say, oh it will be okay and go back to sleep.
- Educate yourself about abuse (read, talk, observe) – and pray!

- Take care of yourself. Put yourself first. You are in a critical place.
- Believe that the God of the Universe can and wants to help you.
- Start by naming five (a handful) of gratitudes every day. It will help you to get through.
- Build on these gratitudes, adding joys, adding ambition, new ideas.
- You will rise, as it were, from the grave, if you keep taking steps forward.

Besides the abuse in some homes, there are other things that can eat and chew away at our happiness and well-being. In this world there are all kinds of things that keep us down. Everything from corruption we hear about in the news or in our neighborhoods, to the fast pace of life around us, to pollution in the air or the additives and alterations in our food; all bombard our brains, and we wonder why we feel the way we do.

Whether you have been brainwashed by an abuser or just plain run down due to life's difficulties, decide today to make some healthy and positive life changes.

There are many healthy adjustments one can make. Eating more healthy, finding enjoyable ways to get exercise and sunshine, associate with people who are positive and happy, find an enjoyable hobby, but best of all, begin to discover the richness the Word of God holds for you. It will literally breathe new life into you and help you carry your load and help you out of your desperate situation.

Here are some scriptures to meditate on as you find your way, up and out, of your 'miry clay'.

"I waited patiently for the Lord; and he inclined unto me, and heard my cry. He brought me up also out of an horrible pit, out of the miry clay, and set my feet upon a rock, and established my goings. And he hath put a new song in my mouth, even praise unto our God: many shall see it, and fear, and shall trust in the Lord. Psalm 40:1–3

We are promised 'joy in the morning', though we have weeping at night. Mercies that are new every morning. Lamentations 3:23; Psalm 30:5

Our prayers are held in golden vials, in heaven. Revelation 5:8. What a breathtaking picture!

"And when he had taken the book, the four beasts and four and twenty elders fell down before the Lamb, having every one of them harps, and golden vials full of odours, which are the prayers of saints." Revelation 5:8

Verse 9: "And they sung a new song, saying, Thou art worthy to take the book, and to open the seals thereof: for thou wast slain, and hast redeemed us to God by thy blood out of every kindred, and tongue, and people, and nation."

# Fear Not ... Isaiah 41:10

Fear paralyzes, imprisons, causes mental and physical illnesses and is very debilitating. Hopelessness, panic, feeling of losing control and a feeling of going crazy can result.

There is also a healthy fear that is there for a good reason. You wouldn't just walk into oncoming traffic or step off a cliff. A healthy fear keeps you safe and from trouble.

Abusive, controlling people have ways to inflict terror on their victims in order to control them. First they build trust. This way they learn the weaknesses of their potential victim. They learn what their victim loves or hates and what makes them afraid. Once the victim has trusted them and told all, then they are ready to control the victim like a thermostat. This is a terrible place to be in for anyone. You cannot turn the clock back and un-tell all you have told the abuser about yourself. One thing you can do is to overcome your fears and get yourself out of the situation. As long as the abuser acts this way, it is not safe to be around them.

If you have been raised to believe that separation and divorce is the unpardonable sin or if you are too prideful to admit to a problem then you might be stuck in the situation for a very long time. If you are too scared to ask for help and hide your problem, it might be impossible to walk away unscathed.

When you marry, you make vows before God and these witnesses to stay together till death do you part. A certain death happens to an abusive marriage. It is not the time to question the philosophy books or how to hold a marriage together that is no longer a marriage but a controlling prison. It is not the time to weep and wail over what you had no control over. If your child were drowning in the deep end of the pool you would not phone your pastor to see if it is a good idea to rescue your child. You wouldn't even care if you could swim well enough. You would just do what needs to be done.

We may make promises and vows and even sign leases and agreements, but sadly sometimes deals are broken. Even God who is perfect and completely sinless, breaks deals He has made. He changes His mind when He sees how sinful we are. He also forgives sins of the worst kind when we are repentant.

There are many marriages that could be saved with God's help, but when you are married to an abuser it's time to jump into the deep end and save your children and yourself from harm.

"Do not make friends with a hot-tempered person, do not associate with one easily Angered." Proverbs 22:24

"Fear not for I am with you; be not dismayed; for I am thy God: I will strengthen thee; yea, I will help thee; yea, I will uphold thee with the right hand of my righteousness." Isaiah 41:10

"God is our refuge and strength, a very present help in trouble." Psalm 46:1

In God are all the answers to all our dilemmas. He reaches out to anyone who will reach to Him and He says ... "Fear not for I am with you..."

_____

_____

_____

_____

## Forget the Former Things

> "Forget the former things; do not dwell in the past.
> See I am doing a new thing! Now it springs up;
> do you not perceive it? I am making a way in the
> desert and streams in the wasteland."
> Isaiah 43:18–19

Do not look back. Do not regret. You have chosen the path you did. It may seem like a mistake but God is never at a loss with our mistakes. It is His plan to give us freedom of choice, and nothing we do ever baffles Him.

If it seems your path is rockier than you expected – give all your pain, worries and cares to God. He can straighten it all out to be better than ever. The key is – give it all to Jesus.

He will take your choices, whatever they are and do a new thing in you! It will be like springs in the desert what He will do; like flowers in springtime; new life in place of the old.

If you've married an abuser, give your spouse to the Lord. Don't tackle the problem on your own. You may need to walk away to keep your sanity. It is a major decision and one that feels like it will kill you. The decision to stay may kill your spirit too. In either case, dealing with abuse is not for the faint of heart. Even if you feel too weak to handle either staying or leaving, make your decision and leave the results to God. Do not look back but whatever you do, give it over to God and let Him make something good out of your life.

Printed in Canada